FD

ENGINE 313 & LADDER 164

Robert Bingham

Valley Press
304 Jean Place
Vienna VA 22180

Copyright 2015, Valley Press
Printed in the United States of America

Library of Congress Cataloging-in-Publication Data

Bingham, Robert C.

ISBN 0974844721
1. Fire Extinction - suppression
TH9145.B562004
628.9'25-dc20

This book is dedicated to the firefighters of Engine 313
and Ladder 164 who have served through the years.

PREFACE

Little has been written about what firehouse life was like back in the 1950s and how the FDNY operated in this era, and the "greatest generation" firemen who served.

My family moved from Manhattan to the Douglaston section of Queens when I was about five years old and luckily we lived about six blocks from the firehouse. I started hanging around the firehouse as soon as I was able to cross Northern Boulevard by myself. That began my life long love of the fire service and the FDNY. At first I was not allowed in the station and hung around outside listening to and counting the bells for incoming alarms. The first time I got inside the firehouse was when the circus was on TV, which was a novelty back then and one of the firemen thought that I would like to see the circus. I would occasionally check the trash cans for interesting stuff like old assignment cards or orders which I took home and studied.

Around that time I bought a Hallicrafters short wave radio that picked up FDNY dispatch. When a call came in for Douglaston, I would hop on my bike and go to the fire. If I wasn't near the radio I could hear the sirens and catch the call, because of the time delay in the announcement. If I was out and about with my friends, I would race to the station and the location would be written in chalk on the blackboard at the watch desk. There would either be a box number for a pull box or an address for a phone alarm.

My dream job was to join the FDNY but that did not happen. The tests were held every four years and I just missed one. One afternoon I went into Engine 313 and the house watchman told me that he had just read in the Firefighter Union Magazine that Washington D. C. was hiring firefighters. I thought that not being from Washington I probably wouldn't have a chance, but I took the tests anyway. I was fortunate to be appointed quickly to the Washington D.C. Fire Department (DCFD).

By the time the next FDNY exam came, I had four years on the job, had married, had a child, bought a house and was studying for promotion, so I never even took the test. I have no regrets, I had a great career with the DCFD, eventually retiring as a Deputy Chief after a 31 year career. Walking into Engine 313 at that moment changed the whole course of my life.

Through the years I have collected many memories, pictures and information about these two companies and I believe that it is time to share this story before it is lost in time.

Writing this book allowed me go back to those golden days at Engine 313 and the firemen that I loved and respected. Almost all of the firemen have since passed away, but in writing this book and reliving my experiences with them I have brought them alive again in a way.

CHAPTERS

CHAPTER 1

DOUGLASTON

Douglaston is an upscale and wealthy neighborhood in the New York City Borough of Queens. It may be the wealthiest single family house neighborhood in the city. It is located in the northeast corner of Queens near the border with Nassau County. The Long Island Railroad which ran from Manhattan to Great Neck in 1874 was instrumental in the development of Douglaston.

The map below shows the location of Douglaston and the surrounding neighborhoods of Bayside, Little Neck and Glen Oaks. Douglaston Manor is a peninsula in Douglaston that is very exclusive with water views, and the homes in the manor sell for well over a million dollars. All the neighborhoods shown are primarily residential, however Glen Oaks has many garden apartments which are mostly two story multiple dwellings. The major streets, Northern Boulevard, Bell Boulevard and UnionTurnpike are mostly commercial. The Long Island Expressway (LIE) runs east and west and the Cross Island Parkway (CIP) is shown running north and south.

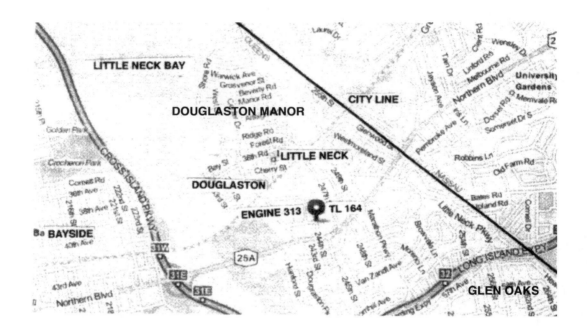

The collage above gives an idea of the composition of Douglaston.

CHAPTER 2

ENGINE 313 & HOOK AND LADDER 164 ARE ESTABLISHED

In the years after the Douglaston and Little Neck volunteer companies were established, the population of New York City exploded. James (Gentleman Jim) Walker was the colorful mayor from 1926 until forced to resign in 1932. The initial years of his mayoralty were a prosperous time for the city, with many public works projects including many firehouses. An astounding 41 new firehouses were placed in service between 1927 and 1931. These new firehouses were known at the time as "Walker Houses," 25 of these houses including Engine 313 were identical, and the other 16 were very similar in design.

In 1924 before the establishment of Engine 313, Engine 306 and Hook and Ladder 152 were placed in service in Bayside, replacing the Bayside volunteer engine and ladder companies. These companies responded to Douglaston to back up the volunteer companies until Engine 313 and H&L164 were established.

Engine 313 and Hook and Ladder 164 went into service in 1929, seven years after a Engine Company 205 in Brooklyn made the last run by a horse-drawn engine.

The installation of Engine 313 and Hook & Ladder 164

Saturday Evening, November 30, 1929
244th Street, Douglaston,
New York, Borough of Queens

THE CEREMONY

The mustering out of Douglaston Hose Company #1 and Active Hook, Ladder and Hose Company #1 of Little Neck and the installation of the paid department took place on Saturday night, November 30, 1929 at the new firehouse and at the Zion Church parish hall.

SPEAKERS:

Honorable James J. Walker - Mayor of New York City
Honorable John J. Dorman - Fire Commissioner of New York City
Honorable George U. Harvey - President; Borough of Queens

Rev. John A. Bohag - Saint Anastasias Church, Douglaston, N.Y.
Rev. Lester Leake Riley - Zion Episcopal Church, Douglaston, N.Y.

PROGRAM

MUSTERING OUT OF VOLUNTEER FIREMEN
LITTLE NECK — DOUGLASTON COMPANIES

1903 - 1929

and

The installation of a Company from the paid Fire Department

Saturday Evening, November 30, 1929

244th Street, Douglaston, New York

Borough of Queens

SPEAKERS

Honorable James J. Walker.............................*Mayor of New York City*

Honorable John J. Dorman..........*Fire Commissioner of New York City*

Honorable George U. Harvey..................*President; Borough of Queens*

Rev. John A. Bohag.............*St. Anastasia's Church, Douglaston; N.Y.*

Rev. Lester Leake Riley.......*Zion Episcopal Church, Douglaston; N.Y.*

Rev. Luther F. Gerhart......*Christ Lutheran Church, Little Neck; N.Y.*

Rev. M. Eugene Flipse.............*Community Church, Douglaston; N.Y.*

Rev. Harold Pattison................*Community Church, Little Neck; N.Y.*

MUSTERING OUT COMMITTEE

Isaac P. Robinson; *Chairman*

Arthur J. McNamara	Hon. Denis O'Leary
Charles Brown, Jr.	Thomas L. Mortimer
William Hutton, Jr.	William Kershaw
James Cummings	Frank D. Hutton
Gilbert Leek	Charles F. Mangan

Ruben Kaiser

Mayor James J. Walker on left and
Fire Commissioner John J. Dorman

The establishment of the Douglaston companies completed the consolidation plan approved thirty-two years earlier and replaced the last of the volunteer companies slated for disbandment. Compared with the six engine and three ladder companies of the paid department in Queens in 1898, there were now fifty-one engines, thirty ladder and one rescue company in the Borough of Queens.

When Engine 313 and Hook and Ladder 164 were placed into service, the FDNY was working an 84 hour week with two platoons. The salary was $3,000 yearly. In 1939 the work week was reduced from 84 hours to 50 hours. In 1953 a 46 hour week was begun which lasted until 1961 when the present 40 hour week was established.

On the following page is a copy of the original order establishing Engine Company 313 and Hook and Ladder 164 at 9 A.M. November 30th, 1929.

FIRE DEPARTMENT

CITY OF NEW YORK

SPECIAL ORDER
No. 215

New York, November 27, 1929

II Transfers, to take effect at 9 A. M., November 30, 1929:

TO ENGINE COMPANY No. 313

Captain *William J. Heffernan*,   Engine 3
Lieutenant *Nathan Perlman*,   "   53

Firemen 1st grade

Frederick W. Koster (Chauffeur),   Engine 32
Joseph C. Miller,   "   "   74
Howard Schaetzle,   "   " 296
James E. Wright,   "   " 307

John J. T. Zwerle, Engine 26   Patrick Duffy,   Engine 204
Louis Hartman,   "   28   John W. Gilday,   "   306
James E. Hawthorne, "   53   Frederick J. Coppers, "   306

Fireman 2nd grade
Harry M. Mahony, Engine 314

TO HOOK AND LADDER COMPANY No. 164

Lieutenant *Joseph J. Fullam*,   H. & L. 14

Firemen 1st grade

Vincent Rooney (Chauffeur),   H. & L. 2
John F. Grimes,   "   "   20
Charles Sammler, Jr., "   "   41
Frederick P.   John T. Sullivan(2), H. & L. 109
     Miller (1), H. & L. 1   Edward S. Boylan,   "   137
William Munda,   "   7   William E. Kroger,   "   152

8

The dedication plaque on the front of Engine 313

The plaque reads:

JAMES J. WALKER - MAYOR
JOHN J. DORMAN - FIRE COMMISSIONER
JOSEPH M. HANNON
CHARLES W. JANNICKY
DEPUTY FIRE COMMISSIONERS
JOHN KENLON - CHIEF OF DEPARTMENT
JOHN DAVEN - DEPUTY CHIEF BROOKLYN AND QUEENS
HUBERT TRACEY - BUREAU OF REPAIRS AND SERVICES

Life in 1929

Herbert Hoover was inaugurated as 31st President of the United States

Eleven years had passed since World War 1 and World War 2 was twelve years away

The Wall Street Crash the most devastating stock market crash in U. S. history began one month before the opening of Engine 313

A U.S. Coast Guard vessel sank a Canadian schooner suspected of carrying liquor during prohibition

The Philadelphia Athletics won the World Series Championship

Jones Beach opened in New York

Prices:

Average house: $7,809.00

Average car: $265.00

Gallon of Gas: .22¢

CHAPTER 3

THE DOUGLASTON VOLUNTEER
FIRE DEPARTMENT

The vote to unite the five boroughs into one city was approved by the residents of Brooklyn, Queens, Staten Island, the Bronx and Manhattan in a citywide referendum in 1895. At the time of annexation in 1898, Queens had some factories in the west and sprawling farms in the east.

At the time there were nine paid companies in the Long Island City Fire Department and seventy-five volunteer companies in seventeen departments with more than two thousand members.

The officers and members of the Long Island City Department became members of the FDNY, and the volunteer companies were to continue on under the supervision of the Chief of Department until replaced by the paid department.

During July 1903, about forty residents of Douglaston associated themselves together as a Fire Corporation, for the suppression of fires in the third ward of the Borough of Queens. The duration of the corporation was to be for a period of fifty years unless prior to that time its duties were assumed by the paid fire department of the City of New York.

Application for a charter was filed August 18,1903 and was approved by the Supreme Court, Fire Commissioner and the Mayor of the City of New York. At this time the affluent Douglaston residents raised sufficient funds to purchase a hose cart and build a firehouse. The temporary first quarters of the company was located just south of the railroad tracks on Main Avenue (now 235 Street) and was used until early in 1906 when the permanent firehouse (still standing) was completed.

THE OPENING CELEBRATION

Members of the newly organized Douglaston Hose company held a celebration on Friday night, July 10, 1903. A reception was held at the Evans Hotel located at 244th Street and Broadway (now Northern Boulevard). Guests included the Ditstler Hose Company and the Bayslde, Little Neck and Flushing Fire Departments.

At the formation of the fire company the president, the Honorable Denis O'Leary was a charter member. He was a prominent politician who was U. S. Congressman and was a founding officer of the Douglaston Fire Department Hose Company No. 1.

The Douglaston Hose Company No. 1 firehouse, note the bell tower in rear

Photo courtesy of the Douglaston Historical Society

A parade in Douglaston celebrated the establishment of the Douglaston Volunteer Fire Department. On July 11, 1903 the Douglastonlans formed at the Long Island Railroad Depot and marched to the Creek Bridge on Broadway (Northern Blvd). There they were met by the Ditstler Hose Company of Jamaica and a newly refurbished hose cart was then formally transferred to the Douglaston Hose Company. The procession back to Douglaston was led by a band and joined by visiting fire companies with their apparatus including the Enterprise Hook and Ladder Company of Bayslde, the Bayside Engine Company, Young America Hose of Flushing and the Active Ladder of Little Neck.

The parade proceeded along Main Avenue to the Evans Hotel. G. F. McKenna and Richard Warren marched in front of the parade setting off fireworks. The parade route was a blaze of light from it's beginning and through the Manor. The train depot was decorated with streamers and a silk banner with the word "Welcome." Practically every residence along the route was decorated with flags, bunting and lanterns.

The ceremonies held at the Evans Hotel lasted until considerably after midnight and included speeches and vaudeville entertainment, followed by refreshments.

Rev. Albert E. Bentley, County Judge Harrison, and the Chief of the Jamaica Fire Department were among the speakers. Vaudeville entertainment included singing, clog dancing and improvisations. Walter S. Faddis, foreman of the Douglaston Hose Company was the master of ceremonies.

The newly organized Douglaston Hose Company hose cart was hand drawn until 1910. Later the hose cart was replaced by a two horse cart.

A period hand drawn hose cart

A period two horse hose cart

The Douglaston Hose Company No. 1 with their two horse hose cart
October 8, 1912
Photo courtesy of the Douglaston Historical Society

The two horse cart was in use until 1918, when a Ford chassis was purchased and the horse drawn cart was mounted on it. The work of transferring the body of the hose cart was performed by members of the company under the supervision of the then Foreman George W. Graham.

This motorized hose cart served until August 1921 when a modern Brockway American La France combination hose and chemical wagon was purchased at a cost of approximately $7,500. This piece of apparatus was augmented by a Mack Hose wagon loaned by the City of New York. This apparatus was in service until 1929, when the Douglaston Hose Company was disbanded.

The following page shows a 1923 photo of the Douglaston Hose Brockway American La France hose and chemical wagon.

The Brockway American LaFrance Wagon
Photo courtesy of the Douglaston Historical Society

The Douglaston Hose Company No. 1, circa 1928
Photo courtesy of the Douglaston historical society

Only twice during the life of the company was it necessary to make direct appeal to the residents for contributions, once in 1921 when the Brockway American LaFrance was purchased, then again in 1923. The company was partially maintained by the City of New York which appropriated $800.00 annually. This was about fifty percent of the cost of maintenance, the balance being made up by the members through the payment of dues and the proceeds of the annual minstrel entertainment.

TRUMPETS

Trumpets were used for two purposes. Working trumpets were used by chief officers to shout orders in the years before portable radios, and a presentation trumpet was awarded to a company or an individual for an outstanding performance.

Trumpet insignias today are used to show the rank of a fire department officer.

There was much rivalry between the volunteer departments. There were often contests such as first water or speed of hose line placements, etc. The Douglaston trumpet below shows that the Douglaston Hose won such a competition.

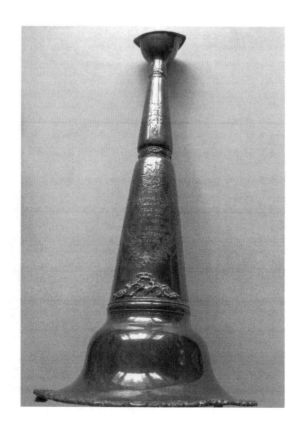

This trumpet reads:

Won at Little Neck
by Douglaston Hose Company No. 1
Hook and Ladder Contest
100 Yards 29 4/5 Seconds
July 4th 1903

The volunteer fire companies were not all work, there were many shows, banquets and fun times. At monthly meetings many interesting and amusing topics were discussed.

An article from the Flushing Daily Times, January 2l, l904:

The Douglaston Hose Company sponsored a dance and entertainment at Literary Hall last night. The event was attended by firemen from Bayside, Flushing, College Point and Jamaica. The hall was decorated with American flags and a flag with the legend "Douglaston Hose Company No. l." The musical entertainment, lasting until 10:30 P.M. was followed by dancing until 1 A.M. when the grand supper march began. After supper, dancing resumed until 4 A.M.

Wow! A grand supper march and dancing all night, quite a celebration.

MINSTREL SHOW

and DANCE

by the

Douglaston Hose Company

THURSDAY AND FRIDAY EVENINGS

APRIL 21 and 22, 1927

PARISH HALL

DOUGLASTON, L. I.

PROGRAM

OVERTURE

ADDRESS BY THE HON. DENIS O'LEARY, *President*

OPENING CHORUS

Ho! People — Ho! People, we're here once again,
All we hope is that you'll have a good time.
Our songs are recent, our jokes they are new,
And it's our ambition to give you all an exhibition
Of singing that's tuneful, of fun that's sublime;
Dancing, too, is on the program tonight — So
    Cheer up, Boys — Wake up, Boys,
And all get set for mirth and laughter.
People, Ho! — People, Hello!

1. There's a Rainbow Around My Shoulder....WARREN DEMLIN
2. Where the Shy Little Violets Grow .... VICTOR REIS
3. My Blackbirds Are Bluebirds Now .... LLOYD GERSBACH
4. Specialty .... EDGAR C. EARLE
5. I Can't Give You Anything But Love .... KEN PAGE
6. All By Yourself in the Moonlight .... BILLIE OBERER
7. Harmonica Duo .... MIKE FLYNN AND BOB DOUGHERTY
8. Down Among the Sugar Cane .... KEN DEMLIN
9. Woodman, Woodman, Spare that Tree .... JACK MORTIMER
10. Saxophone Specialty .... LLOYD GERSBACH
11. Blue Grass .... DICK O'TOOLE
12. Those Wedding Bells Are Breaking Up that
    Old Gang of Mine .... TOM FOWLER
13. Button Up Your Overcoat .... FRANK MORTIMER

CLOSING CHORUS

Good Night, you people, we bid you Good-Bye,
Hoping that our show has pleased you tonight.
Tell your good neighbors, the Boys are all right,
That they made you happy,
That their songs are good and snappy,
We say — Good-Bye, folks — we say it ruefully,
'Cause we love to have you with us always — So
Don't forget — don't go yet,
There's good music for your dancing.
People, Ho! — People, Good-Bye.

Certificates were presented to members of the department to honor their service

Photo Courtesy of the Douglaston Historical Society

ALARMS

In 1905 the New York Fire Department installed fire alarm boxes in Douglaston and Little Neck to improve the reporting of fires. All boxes were locked and the keys placed with three members of the fire company who lived nearby. In that era boxes were locked to prevent false alarms and keys were given to responsible people living near the fire box. Interestedly some 60 years later in 1976, there were 285,290 false alarms in New York City. Needless to say, the fire alarm boxes were not locked.

After the installation of the telegraph fire alarm, charts were distributed by the fire company showing the number and location of the fire alarm boxes. When an alarm of fire was sounded from a fire alarm box, the bell in fire bell tower in rear of the firehouse tolled the number of the fire alarm box from which the alarm was sounded.

At the outset the alarms were rare, averaging twenty or thirty a year but alarms eventually increased to more than one hundred a year.

DOUGLASTON HOSE CO. No. 1

ALARM SYSTEM

DOUGLASTON

Box Location

21	Bay Ave.—Beach Pl.
23	Centre Drive—Knollwood Ave.
24	East Drive—Grosvenor St.
25	Centre Drive—Manor Road
26	East Drive—Arleigh Road
27	Centre Drive—Ridge Road
28	East Drive—Hillside Ave.
31	Main Ave.—Hillside Ave.
32	Cherry St.—Circle Road
34	Main Ave.—Willow St. Community Church
41	Poplar St.—Prospect Ave. School Annex
42	Pine St.—Orient Ave.
43	Main Ave.—Pine St.
51	Douglaston Inn—245th St.
52	Broadway—Alley Road

Compliments of

P. A. BRUNING

The Quality
GROCER

Fruits & Vegetables

Northern Blvd. and
244th Street

Douglaston, N. Y.

Phones:
Bayside 1571-1572

LITTLE NECK

Box Location

61	Little Neck Dock
63	Cutter Ave. & Bayview Westmoorland
65	Opposite Little Neck Depot
67	Public School No. 94
69	Old House Landing Road
71	Floral Park Road, near East Alley Road
72	Broadway—Clinton Ave. Opp. Little Neck Fire House
73	Clinton Ave.—East Alley Road
74	Clinton Ave.—Halfway bet. Broadway and East Alley Road
75	Browvale Drive & Highland Ave., Little Neck Hills
78	Broadway—Old House Landing Road
79	Opposite old school house Floral Park Road

IN CASE OF FIRE do not delay in sending in an alarm. To send in an alarm, open box with key on handle. Pull hook inside all the way down and let go, or telephone Fire Headquarters, JAMAICA 8080 and give nearest fire box, as per list above, or your exact location. After giving alarm, wait at box, until apparatus arrives to direct firemen. By so doing, you will greatly oblige

DOUGLASTON HOSE COMPANY, No 1

Charles Mangan, Foreman

The residents were instructed on how to report a fire:

IN CASE OF FIRE

Do not delay in sending in an alarm. Open the box
with key and pull the hook inside all the way down.
After giving alarm, wait at box, to direct the firemen.

The Douglaston Hose Company Badge
Photo courtesy of the Douglaston Historical Society

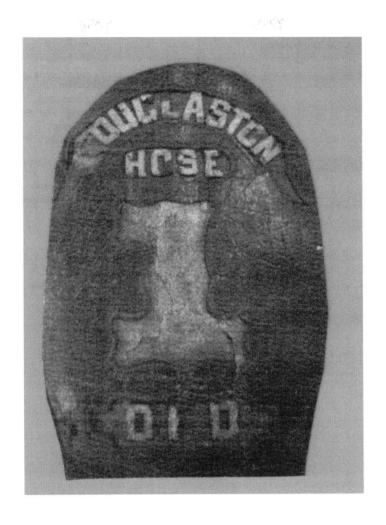

The Douglaston Hose Company Frontispiece
Photo courtesy of the Douglaston Historical Society

CHAPTER 4

THE ACTIVE HOOK, LADDER AND HOSE COMPANY OF LITTLE NECK

After several disastrous fires in the communities of both Little Neck and Douglaston, the public spirited citizens of the community of Little Neck, discussed the possibility of organizing a volunteer fire department for the protection of life and property.

At a meeting at John Flynn's Hotel near the Little Neck Railroad Station on February 27, 1901, Hook, Ladder and Hose Company No. 1 of Little Neck was organized. This was two years before the establishment of the Douglaston Fire Company.

Incorporation of this company was approved several years later in 1903 by Thomas Sturgis, Fire Commissioner of the City of New York, Seth Low, Mayor of the City of New York (an early fireboat was named for him)and G. J. Garretson, Justice of the Supreme Court of the State of New York.

On November 21, 1901, David L.Van Nostrand offered a temporary site for the erection of a firehouse which was accepted. In 1901 the material for the erection of the first firehouse on the Van Nostrand site was furnished gratis by John Stuart, a well known builder in the community. This firehouse was occupied by the fire company until the erection of the replacement firehouse, located at Clinton Avenue (now Marathon Parkway) and Northern Boulevard. In 1902, a hand-drawn piece of fire apparatus was purchased by the members, which was the pride of the countryside. This piece of apparatus had a hand pump attachment which required the brawn of young and alert firemen to operate. The apparatus was also equipped with leather water buckets which were used to carry water from nearby streams or wells to extinguish fire, no water mains being in the community at that time. This mode of firefighting was hard work, as great and constant exertion was necessary throughout the duration of the fire.

The erection and completion of the new firehouse was completed in 1905. After moving into the new firehouse with the hand drawn apparatus, it was found that the needs of the community required a more modern piece of firefighting apparatus, and in the same year a horse drawn piece of apparatus was purchased by the company.

There being no telegraph fire alarm system in the community in 1902, it was necessary to travel on foot, horseback or by some other conveyance to the firehouse, in front of which was a bell which was rung by the person giving an alarm of fire. Upon the arrival of the firemen at the firehouse, directions were furnished and the firemen proceeded to the scene of the fire with their apparatus.

The fire company was a very active one, having on its rolls sixty members who were connected with many of the well known families along the North Shore. The work performed by these members was necessary and important and provided an effective firefighting organization to serve the community.

The Active Hook & Ladder Company Badge

No. 84—Fire House, Little Neck, L. I.   P. L. GREGORY

The Little Neck Firehouse
Photos courtesy of the Douglaston Historical Society

CHAPTER 5

THE END OF THE VOLUNTEER FIRE COMPANIES

On November 30th, 1929, the last day of the Douglaston and Little Neck Volunteer Fire Departments there was a parade celebrating the arrival of the New York City paid fire department.

Parade Formation

The parade formed at the corner of Northern Boulevard and Clinton Avenue, (Marathon Parkway) and extended north on Clinton Avenue in the following formation and which started promptly at 2 P.M.

Police Escort
N.Y. City Fire Department Band
N.Y. City officials
Flushing Parental School Band
Flushing Exempt Firemen's Association
Port Washington Fire Department Flower Hill Company
Alert Fire Department Band
Alert Fire Department of Great Neck
Manhasset Lakeville Fire Department
Vigilant Fire Department of Great Neck
Douglaston & Little Neck Band
Douglaston Hose Co. No. 1
Little Neck Active Hook, Ladder and Hose Company

Line of March

From Clinton Avenue to Northern Blvd through and around Douglaston Manor back to Northern Blvd to 244th Street to the new city firehouse. The apparatus then turned right at 244th Street and parked in side streets on the south side of Northern Blvd. The men turned left at 244th Street and marched to the new firehouse and lined up for the ceremony.

After the ceremonies, visiting firemen were served refreshments at the Little Neck Firehouse.

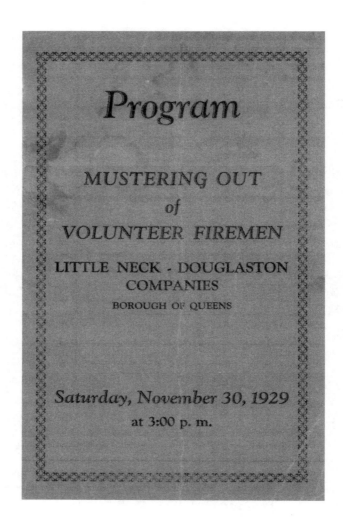

Program

MUSTERING OUT
of
VOLUNTEER FIREMEN

LITTLE NECK - DOUGLASTON
COMPANIES
BOROUGH OF QUEENS

Saturday, November 30, 1929
at 3:00 p. m.

The program for mustering out the volunteer firemen
Little Neck - Douglaston companies
1903-1929
Program courtesy of the Douglaston Historical Society

The Douglaston Fire Company as well as the Active Hook & Ladder Co. No. I of Little Neck, worked together and always enjoyed the confidence of the residents of the district who appreciated the voluntary services rendered.

The volunteer fire departments of Douglaston and Little Neck provided fire protection for nearly thirty years. The citizens were grateful and proud of their services as shown by the following testimonial.

<u>A Tribute to our firemen from the Douglaston Civic Association</u>

The members of the Volunteer Fire Departments of Douglaston and Little Neck are mustered out tonight, and regular firemen of the City of New York take their places. To the outgoing group we give our tribute of appreciation, and to the new, we extend our warm greetings of welcome.

To our own faithful volunteers we are especially appreciative of their sacrifice and devotion to the protection of our homes. Every man, when he volunteered, subjected himself to danger to say nothing of the personal sacrifice of monthly meetings attended when other engagements would have been more pleasurable. Their sacrifice has been for us, to protect our homes, our property and even our lives.

As representatives of the community, therefore, we give this inadequate tribute to all of the men of the Douglaston Hose Company and the Active Hook, Ladder and Hose Company of Little Neck, and we extend greeting and welcome to our new protectors.

The certificate replicated below was presented to Fireman William McCurdy upon the disbanding of the Douglaston Volunteer Fire Company.

The certificate reads:

FROM THE TOWNSPEOPLE OF DOUGLASTON

William B. McCurdy

DOUGLASTON HOSE COMPANY NO. 1
DOUGLASTON, LONG ISLAND, NEW YORK

You have stood as a protector of our homes, our property, and our lives from devastating fires. During the long years when our community was without city fire department protection, you have responded as a volunteer in glad and efficient service.

Day and night, in rain and snow, stifling summer and bitter cold, disregarding personal comfort, you have answered the fire bells call. Your attendance at meetings, fire drills and hose practice on equipment secured through your efforts, is a noble example in our midst.

You have shown a splendid spirit in your service for the community. On our hearts, appreciation is written large of which this slight token is but a symbol.

The new city station replaced the Volunteer Douglaston Hose 1, whose building is still standing and located at 42-28 235 Street near the Long Island Railroad station.

The Douglaston Volunteer Firehouse now occupied by the American Legion

Hook and Ladder 164 replaced the Active Little Neck Hook and Ladder Company which was the last volunteer truck company in the city. The volunteer house was converted into a bank for many years, and was then demolished about 25 years ago. A McDonald's restaurant now occupies this site at Northern Boulevard and Marathon Parkway.

CHAPTER 6

THE FIREHOUSE

A firehouse represents a great deal more than a structure. The firehouse is looked upon by many firefighters as part of their lives. It is not just a place to go to work, but is their second home. This has special meaning for firefighters, and creates a strong camaraderie among them.

Engine 313's original apparatus doors were painted green, were steel and opened horizontally riding on tracks in the cement. They never worked right as the small motor could not open and shut the super heavy doors for long before breaking down, so for many years they were opened and closed manually. The entrance door to the firehouse was a small door in the apparatus door, an obvious safety hazard since you could be entering through the doors while the doors were opening. This was long before OSHA, they would have loved it.

In the 1950s a handball court was constructed on the south side of the building. It was used by the firefighters for a long time. When homes were built next to the firehouse it was necessary to install doors in the court wall to allow cars to pass through, which had previously parked where the new houses were built.

 In the rear yard there was a concrete pit built so you could pull your car up on the ramp and work under it in the pit. Through the years there were various orders given to fill it in as one could fall in, but that did not seem to happen.

The sitting room, used as a relaxing and dining area originally had a high ceiling, which now has had a dropped ceiling installed. Meals were eaten on a wooden picnic table. The chairs were what was known as "the firehouse chair" since they were commonly used in firehouses.

Originally there was a separate kitchen next to the sitting room. In time the wall was taken down to make one large room. Recently a big screen TV room with lounge chairs was built in the old handball area.

Back then the basement was just one large vacant and open area with a coal chute and a coal storage area needed to maintain heat during the cold winter months. A typical coal delivery was listed as "received 24,000 pounds of buckwheat coal." In winter the fire had to be tended to keep the coal burning 24 hours a day. The coal ashes were white in color and very heavy. Periodically they were shoveled into large metal trash cans and hauled by rope up through the doors in the apron in front of the firehouse for disposal.

The Douglaston firehouse in the 1950s shown with the original doors

Over time the basement became a physical fitness room, a study center and workshop. Likewise the bunk-room that was an open area of bunks surrounded by lockers on the walls has since been changed to a separate room for bunks and another for lockers, reducing noise.

The hose tower was used to hang up hose to dry until the tower was no longer needed. Now, pressed for space, a floor was installed that is even with the apparatus floor and now houses soda machines.

The watch desk originally was open, with no walls or roof. In the early 1950s it was enclosed with plywood to provide screening and eventually air conditioning. Like many firehouses at the time the box numbers and locations that E313 & L164 ran were listed on a very large board on the wall behind the watch desk.

All the house activities were recorded in a big black desk journal. Everything was documented, the arrival and departure times of each member entering or leaving quarters, the subject of all correspondence coming or going, and even deliveries of heating coal. All incoming alarms were recorded, not just the ones that they responded to. Company drills were regular, taken seriously and were recorded.

I have two journals from the 1950s that I have used as background for this book. The journals cover one year between November 1956 and October 1957.

A 1950s watch desk
WNYF Photo

ENGINE 313 FLOOR PLANS 1956

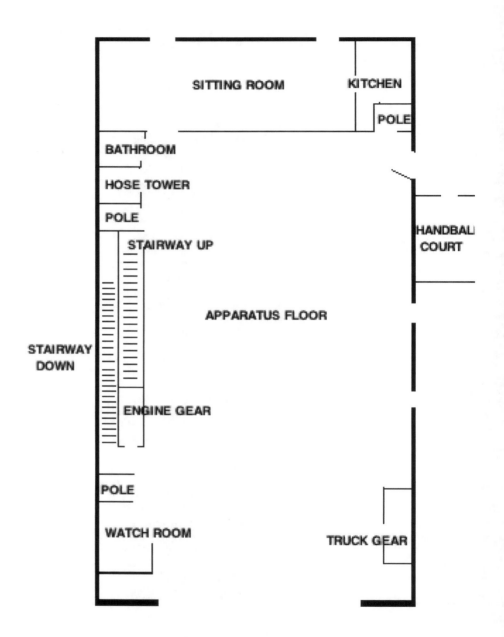

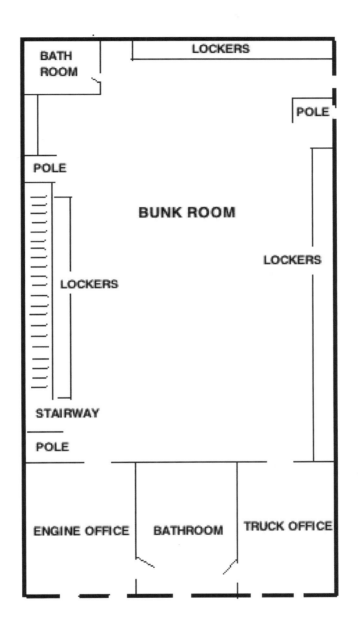

BATH ROOM

LOCKERS

POLE

POLE

BUNK ROOM

LOCKERS

LOCKERS

STAIRWAY

POLE

ENGINE OFFICE

BATHROOM

TRUCK OFFICE

37

CHAPTER 7

THE OFFICERS AND MEN

I knew three of the original firemen who opened the firehouse in 1929. John Gilday was the MPO (motor pump operator) who really knew his district and could be counted on to get water. He was the first fireman to stand watch in the new house. He was known to have swam around Manhattan Island in his younger days.

Another was John J. T. Zwerle a real old timer. He lived in little Neck and smoked a pipe. He also chewed tobacco and when he was on watch and the phone would ring he would spit it all out on the floor. Fortunately the phone didn't ring very often. He said very little and mostly grunted yes or no. He was known as Tonto after the long gone Lone Ranger radio show. Tonto was the Lone Rangers faithful companion who spoke very little and mostly grunted.

The third was Freddie Coppers a sweet older man. I remember a store fire in the dead of winter in Little Neck in the block where the movie used to be. After it was over they put Freddie in the chiefs car with a blanket around him. That was his last fire. After that he was a messenger for the 53rd battalion and he died as an an active fireman a short time later.

Some of the old timers were appointed as far back as 1917, which meant that they worked with horse drawn fire apparatus. Legend has it that the horse drawn era was the golden age of firefighting. According to the old timers there was little romance about working with horses. I was told that they required lots of attention, smelled, produced acres of manure and the meaner ones would bite you if they had the chance. They also complained that the city was more concerned about the welfare of the horses than the men. They said that horses were expensive to buy and firemen came free.

They also complained about the early motorized trucks before electric starters. This was because the engine would have to be hand cranked and sometimes when the engine would start up it would spin the crank handle which could break your arm.

Interestingly, throughout the 1950s and maybe beyond, the apparatus wheels were washed with a bucket and brush after every run. This was originally done to clean the horse manure from the streets off the wheels. The guys would say that the horses were gone but the horse manure remained.

I really enjoyed hanging around the watch desk. The firemen on watch back then had no TV, radio or phones and had to sit for three hour stretches. Because of this I got to know and become friends with many of them. They would love to talk about the old days, fires long past, their lives and the characters that they had worked with, which as a teen I ate up.

Engine 313 and Hook & Ladder 164 circa 1952

The 1950s firemen were a great bunch and they were my heroes. I can still see their faces. In time, some of the firemen became mentors to me especially Charlie Rowan and Joe Andrulis and I became friends with many others. One fireman friend and his wife came to my home to visit with me and my parents. Another invited me on a camping trip with his family and yet another wanted me to take his daughter to her high school prom, which I stupidly did not do.

A few of the more memorable firemen included Frank Baxter, who was appointed to Ladder 164 in 1938 and retired in 1958 and was probably the only one to ever be appointed to and retire from L164, Lieutenant "Wild Bill" Hyland a really fun guy, Bill Corrigan an old timer who had survived several building collapses in Manhattan which caused him to walk a little bent over, Arthur (Tiny) Donaldson a 250 pound comedian, "Country" Jim Owens, from Tennessee who read western novels non-stop. Lieutenant John J. Hamilton H & L 164 was an old timer who would fascinate me with stories of fires he fought in Manhattan in the early days. Another was Mario Cherchi, a very efficient lieutenant who retired as a deputy chief and Charlie McKeogh who was a BC in the 53rd battalion. He was quite a character who was much loved and known throughout the job. One of the captains at Engine 313 in that era was Captain Nigro. His son Daniel joined the FDNY and eventually became Chief of Department and is now the current Fire Commissioner.

FIremen from left: Bill Corrigan, Frank Lonegan, John Gilday, and Jim Owens

In the mid fifties the salaries were not as good as they are now. The salary for a first grade firemen was around $6,000 a year. The firehouse parking lot looked more like a junkyard than a new car lot. In those days very few wives worked and almost all the firemen had part time jobs except some of the officers and older firemen. A few of the firemen had a concession to run a boat tender service in Whitestone. I spent the summer working for them running the tender from the dock to customers boats. It was a great summer job for a high school kid. Occasionally I helped them out in a lawn cutting business, not so much fun.

Back then you could buy a basic house in the Douglaston area for about 3 or 4 times a firemen's salary. Firemen in that era often lived near their firehouses. Some of the Douglaston firemen walked to work and others lived nearby in Bayside and towards Flushing. Now with house prices $600,000 and up most firemen live way out on the island. I grew up on 245th Street which used to be home to a few firemen, some cops, and several Con Ed people. Now lawyers and CPA's own the block.

The firemen worked a 46 hour week. The schedule was to work two 9 A.M. to 6 P.M. tours, followed by a day off, then two 6 P.M. to 9 A.M. tours, followed by three days off. Fireman Frank Baxter once told me that under a previous work schedule he was always at the firehouse at 8 A.M., either coming or going unless he was sick or on vacation. There were no trading of days or 24 hour shifts and overtime was very rare. Vacations were for one entire month, and if you were unlucky you vacationed in January.

In those days there were not many company meals, most firemen either ate at home or made their own individual meals. However in nice weather there would often be cookouts out back and a good time was had by all. There was a horseshoe court out back and some of the firemen were really good at it. There would often be singing, people sang back then. I guess it was because most of the men were born around the time of the first World War when folks had little entertainment and singing was popular. Lieutenant Bill Bailey L164 had sung professionally and could sing like a bird. No, he did not sing, "Bill Bailey won't you please come home."

In those years they did not have the company parties, picnics, ball games and social events like there are today. The company social events were mostly for funerals and 20 year parties. I believe that was true citywide. The 20 year parties were thrown by the guy who reached 20 years on the job and became eligible for retirement. The parties always involved food, drink and singing of old time tunes. I attended a few of the 20 year parties which were usually held in a rental hall.

Once following a funeral, Frank and Sully came back to the firehouse with Sully in no condition to go home. It was decided that Frank would call Mrs. Sully. Frank tapped out the number on the locked civil defense phone. The call went like this. "Mrs Sullivan this is Frank, Sully won't be home tonight". Pause. Frank: "Sully is a fine man." Pause, "He is too."

Physical fitness was almost unknown and eating was in. I made countless runs to the candy store on my bike for half pints of ice cream. However most firemen were in pretty good shape from their part time jobs and the handball court. Medical leave was rare and used mostly for serious problems.

Back then there were more older members than now, some were in their sixties, but most of the guys assigned there were in their mid to late 40s and many had come from busy companies. Several of the men had been injured in building collapses during downtown fires. Somebody was always the senior man, but that was not recognized then as it is now.

The company would run short for messenger duty, when daily a fireman would take the mail in what was known as "the bag" to the battalion headquarters and return with new mail.

Sometimes hydrant and building inspections were done by a fireman who would go out by himself. I think that was a carryover from the old days when manning was heavy.

Back in the day there were not a whole lot of standard operating procedures. There were standard evolutions that would show how to stretch a hose line or raise and position a ladder, but what duties companies were responsible for were not well defined. In general companies other than first due reported to the battalion chief to be assigned a job.

Throughout much of the 1950s Ladder 164 did not have a captain, only a lieutenant who was an acting captain. I suppose that it was an economy move. Around that time the city hired an outside efficiency firm to study the fire department. It recommended the closure of many firehouses including Ladder 164. Nobody could believe it. None of the recommended closures happened and during the war years in the 1970s (a period of civil unrest when entire neighborhoods were destroyed by fire), some of the companies that were to be closed had to add second sections to help handle the work load.

There was never any disciplinary action taken during my time. All wasn't peaches and cream, there was a captain in the 1940s who everybody seemed to have hated. There was also the story of a battalion chief who years earlier had quietly glided the chiefs car to the front of quarters so he could run in to catch the watchman smoking. He thought he caught the watchman and he was going to put him on charges until the lieutenant told him that the watchman didn't smoke. Typically, and perhaps because of this, when the battalion chief went on the air, a courtesy call would often be given to all the houses in the battalion saying that the chief was out making his rounds to the firehouses.

One threat of disciplinary action often joked about was the possibility of getting transferred to Engine 151 in the Tottenville section of Staten Island. This firehouse was at the far end of the island and the Verrazano bridge did not exist. To get there from Long Island where most firemen lived, you would have to take the bus to Flushing, ride the subway to Times Square, change to the downtown Battery Park subway. Then a thirty minute ride on the Staten Island ferry before changing to the bus to the end of the island. The trip was over two hours one way, so assignment there would be a huge problem, you would almost have to move to the island to get to work.

The inevitable small problems were handled in house. One problem involved Willy. He was a World War 2 veteran and the war had only been over around 10 years. Willy was a U.S. Marine who went through hell, and came back with what would now be known as post-traumatic stress. He had been in many of the worst battles and once was in a battle where he was the only one in his platoon who was not killed or wounded. He served his country well and he was a great guy, reliable, well liked and helpful, however now and then the stress came through. Willy had a heart of gold, as a teen after I got my first car and had mechanical problems he repaired it for me in the firehouse parking lot.

Many of the Douglaston firemen were appointed around 1938 because shorter hours resulted in hiring many new firemen. This was during the depression and competing for a good steady government job was highly competitive and brought in many bright young guys. In the 1950s, there was sometimes a little conflict between these younger guys and the older officers, many of whom were old school and not as well educated as their younger firemen. It wasn't a big deal but it caused some grumbling now and then.

The test for firemen was very difficult because there were many more applicants than vacancies. The written test and the agility test were of equal weight and more difficult than today. The agility test required applicants to broad jump at least six feet, do sit-up's while holding 40 pound weights behind their necks, scale a 10 foot wall and lift 100 pound weights. Most who were appointed scored 100% on both the written and agility tests.

There were no apparatus accidents during the 1950s that I was aware of. In earlier years I heard the hose wagon accidentally went into reverse instead of drive and damaged the rear tile wall, which was fixed by the guys without paperwork.

Promotions were a big problem in those days. The 1938 guys were affected by World War 2 which greatly limited promotions. After the war, any returning veteran who passed the Lieutenants exam was given absolute preference. This meant that any vet who passed the test jumped ahead of any non-vet, regardless of the mark received. The result was, many of the non-vets who would have been promoted under normal circumstances never had a chance to be promoted to lieutenant for almost 20 years and near until the end of their careers.

CHAPTER 8

APPARATUS AND EQUIPMENT

Upon the opening of the firehouse in 1929, Engine 313 was issued a brand new 1929 American LaFrance 700 GPM pumper and a new Seagrave hose wagon. In that era there were many such two piece companies.

A 1929 American LaFrance Pumper

Eighteen years later in 1947 Engine 313 got a brand new beautiful cab-ahead-of-engine design American LaFrance pumper. It was the first 12 cylinder apparatus in the FDNY. This pumper had seats on either side of the cab forward engine. No one ever used the seats, and it would take 35 years for members to ride inside the fire trucks. Members would ride on the back step hanging onto what were known as subway straps, named after similar straps on the NYC subways. All the apparatus in this era had bells including the chiefs cars. Bells preceded sirens and when sirens came about the bells remained. You see very few bells now, and those around are more for tradition than as warning signal.

Engine 313's 1947 American La France pumper
Photo courtesy of WNYF

The pumpers in those days did not carry water. That seems hard to believe now, but back then many big city fire departments operated the same way. It was likely a carryover from the days when steamers were not able to carry water.

To get water the pumpers would have to connect to a fire hydrant. This required the MPO (motor pump operator) to remove a soft connection hose from the pumper and connect it between the hydrant and the pumper. There was 2 1/2 inch hose, but there were no 1 1/2 inch lines, or pre-connected attack lines. Later there were booster lines for outside fires.

The hose wagon was a 1929 Seagrave, one of fifty that the department purchased that year. The hose wagon originated in the days of steamers which needed a second piece to carry hose, men, tools and appliances. The hose wagons did not have pumps. The steamer was the pump. When motorized pumpers came into service, many engine companies were still kept as two piece companies.

Engine 313's hose wagon had the typical open cab and leather seats. This hose wagon did not have a working siren. The siren was broken for years. Engine 313 was a two piece engine company from inception until the mid 1950's. The FDNY still uses hose wagons as the second piece of engine companies first due at the cities airports.

Fireman Jim Owens on Engine 313's hose wagon

Sometimes Engine 313's hose wagon came in handy, such as at brush fires when the pumper would hit a hydrant and the hose wagon would lay a line from the pumper and position the wagon close to the brush fire.

A 1929 FDNY Seagrave Hose Wagon
Photo from the FASNY Museum of Firefighting

In 2014, Engine 313 received one of the thirty-eight new KME pumpers delivered to the department. The cab has a stainless steel split-tilt cab specifically designed and built to the city's custom requirements. The engine has a 2000 GPM two stage pump, a stainless steel pump and body, and a 500 gallon water tank.

Engine 313's brand new 2014 KME Pumper
Photo by Jimmy Raftery FDNY Dispatcher

A LIST OF ENGINE 313's PUMPERS THROUGH THE YEARS

11/30/29 American LaFrance 700 GPM REG # 6655

11/30/29 Seagrave Hose Wagon REG # 244

6/14/47 American LaFrance 750 GPM REG # 9032

11/16/58 1954 Ward LaFrance Booster 750 GPM REG #3320

6/29/70 1970 Mack 1000 GPM Diesel MP7074

9/17/72 1972 Mack Diesel 1000 GPM MP7215

3/16/81 1980 American LaFrance Century 1000 GPM AP8020

3/23/93 1993 Seagrave 1000 GPM SF9324

4/17/03 2002 Seagrave SP 1000 GPM

12/1/14 2014 KME 2000 GPM

The following collage shows some of the various apparatus used by Engine 313 in past years.

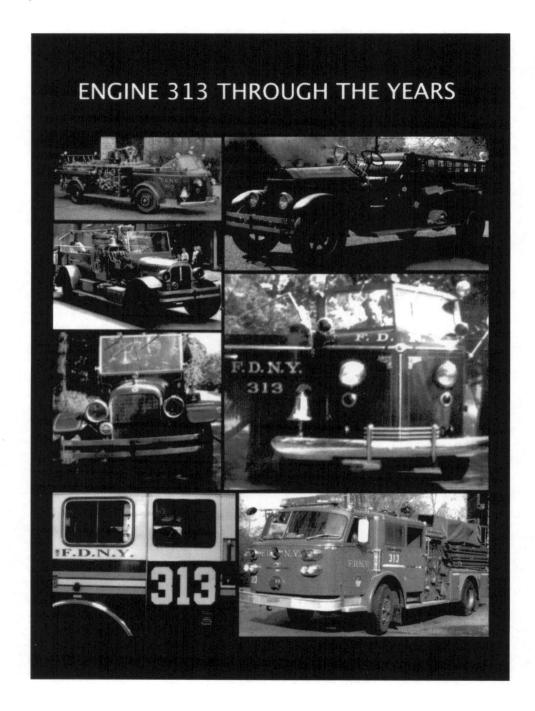

ENGINE 313 THROUGH THE YEARS

HOOK AND LADDER 164

Hook & Ladder I64 started with a 1926 Pierce Arrow City Service truck with a 32 HP engine. This type of truck was a forerunner of the tractor drawn aerials.

A 1926 Pierce Arrow City Service Truck
Photo courtesy of WNYF

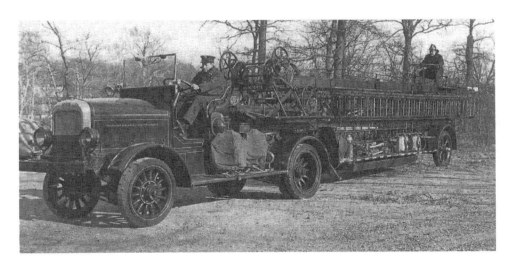

Ladder 164's 1931 FWD Tractor with an 1914 American LaFrance trailer
Photo by John Calderone, courtesy WNYF

LIST OF LADDER APPARATUS RECEIVED THROUGH THE YEARS

9/30/1929 1926 Pierce Arrow City Service (32 HP) 50 foot aerial #246

10/21/36 1931 FWD Tractor with a 1914 American LaFrance trailer 65 foot aerial

12/14/40 1947 WLF Tractor with a 1927 Seagrave trailer 75 foot aerial

6/08/60   1948 WLF Tractor D with a 1941 Seagrave trailer #347

2/23/68   1955 FWD Truck 75 foot aerial #403

7/10/71   1962 Mack Grove Rear Mount 100 foot aerial #456

2/11/72   1962 American LaFrance 100 foot aerial #463

3/01/74   1971 Mack Tower Ladder 75 foot MT 7103

5/04/81   1980 Mack Tower Ladder 75 foot MT 8005

10/25/91 1991 Mack Tower Ladder 95 foot MT 9101

3/02/99   1995 FWD Saulsbury Tower Ladder 75 foot ST9506

5/9/06   2006 Seagrave Aerial-Scope 75 foot tower ladder

The following collage shows some of the various trucks used by Ladder 164 in past years.

HOOK AND LADDER 164 THROUGH THE YEARS

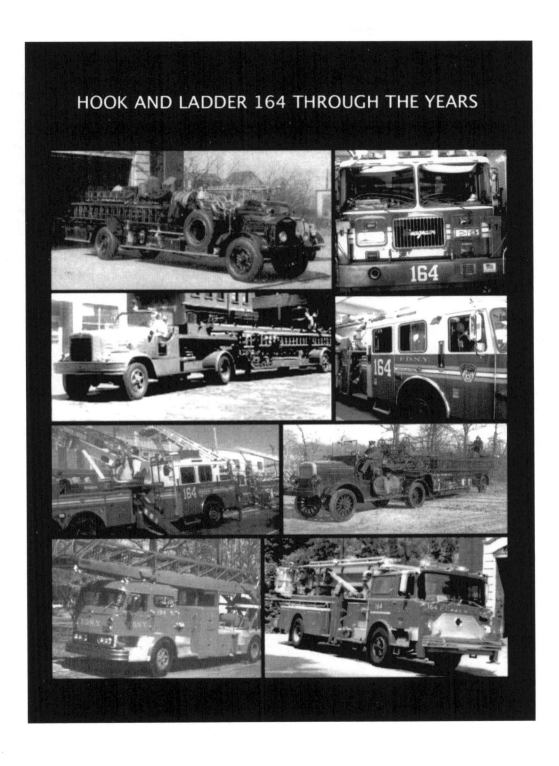

Tower Ladder 164's current truck, a 2006 Seagrave Aerial-Scope
Photo by Jimmy Raftety FDNY Dispatcher

BATTALION CHIEF CARS

The battalion chiefs car in the 53rd battalion was a big DeSoto with a large bell mounted on the front. Below is a typical 1950s Battalion Chiefs car.

APPARATUS SPARE RIGS

Ladder 164 once was assigned a spare apparatus that when it went up a steep hill the men on the side would have to get off and walk alongside so the truck could get up the hill. This really happened you can't make stuff like this up.

The spare apparatus in those days were really old. Engine 313's spare pumper shown below had a chain drive and solid rubber tires.

Engine 313's spare apparatus circa 1950 with Fireman John J.T. Zwerle

APPARATUS WARNING LIGHTS

Now apparatus are all lit up like a Christmas tree. Warning lights in the 1950s were very poor by todays standards. Back then Engine 313's new 1947 American LaFrance featured what was known as a Mars light. It was mounted above the windshield and its red beam rotated back and forth. There were also small fixed red lights mounted on the front of the apparatus and the rear had two small red tail lights.

Hook and Ladder 164 only had a small fixed red light on each fender and the word FIRE painted on the front bumper. At night the officer would often turn on a large spotlight and direct it up and down on the overhead trees to attract the attention of oncoming drivers. The rear of the truck had one small tail light. The truck also had an old red globed kerosene lantern that hung on the back of the truck that was often lit at dusk.

EQUIPMENT

In that era both engine and ladder trucks carried scaling ladders. This ladder can be seen on the top of the spare pumper pictured previously. These ladders were used for rescues beyond the reach of ordinary ladders. The scaling ladder was carried to the top of an aerial or conventional ladder. Then, the scaling ladder, with a big metal hook on one end was swung through the next window above. The fireman would ascend the ladder, straddle the window and swing the ladder into the window above. This was repeated until the victim was reached. This was obviously a very dangerous procedure that was rarely used, but successful rescues were made using this ladder. In those years recruits were trained on these ladders.

A scaling ladder rescue in Manhattan
Photo courtesy of WNYF

Self contained breathing apparatus (SCBA) were introduced in the late 1950s. They were not well received and were mostly kept in their boxes and buried under other stuff on the rigs. The thinking was the the masks could be dangerous because they could get you too deep into buildings and you would lose your sense of where you were. It was thought that they might have a use in a really nasty basement fire. It took about thirty years for the masks to be fully accepted and used and the days of the smoke eaters were over, (mostly).

The protective equipment back in those days was rudimentary. Firemen wore black rubber raincoats which were great to repel water but lousy for protection. The black coat was also hard to see in smoke or at night. The leather helmets were substantial then as now. Boots were the old style pull up types used during that era. The problem with them was that they were seldom pulled up because most fires were not workers, so it was not part of the routine. There were no bunker pants.

There were no portable radios back then, which made inside firefighting an adventure. The early radios came twenty years later and were barely portable and were carried on your back like a big knapsack as shown in this WNYF photo.

The aerial ladders were wooden and were operated by manpower, nothing was hydraulic. When the ladder was up it was manually cranked down by hand against the springs. To raise the ladder the tiller seat and steering wheel had to be removed and the spring would be released causing the ladder to fly up into the air. There were hand cranked control wheels to raise, lower, rotate or extend the ladder as shown.

The life net was a standard piece of equipment on F.D.N.Y. trucks. The life net was used as a last resort to catch people jumping out of burning buildings, however it was very dangerous for both jumpers and firemen. They were removed in the 1960s because in almost any situation in which a life net could be used, a ladder could be placed quicker, with less men, and greater safety.

FDNY life net practice

In the early days of the cold war some pencil pusher decided that the citizens would confuse the air raid sirens with apparatus fire sirens, so sirens were not allowed to be used. Firemen being inventive devised exhaust whistles which were mounted under the apparatus engine. The officer would pull up on a rope and the exhaust whistle would scream really loud and would really get peoples attention. They lasted a few years until sanity prevailed and sirens came back.

CHAPTER 9

FIREHOUSE LIFE

One could often smell brass polish in the fire station. This was due to the regular polishing of the brass tools and appliances as well as the sliding poles. The idea was that polishing and handling the tools regularly would make you familiar with where tools were located and what they were used for, and the poles would look their shiny best.

The dress uniform was very similar to todays, but there was no standard work uniform. The result was a hodgepodge of mostly dungaree pants and mostly blue chambray shirts. This dress seemed acceptable at the time, but looking back it was a rag tag appearance. There were no fire department or company patches anywhere, they didn't come until years later.

The house watchman had to wear a full dress uniform including the uniform hat, I think that the idea was that visitors to the station would be impressed. It was probably a good idea but it didn't work very well. The firehouse was located on a side street not a thru street, and across from a cemetery so very few civilians ever visited the station. The troops obeyed the rule but not the spirit. I think that the same tie was passed from watchman to watchman through the years or at least it looked that way. The middle aged guys who were growing bald used to complain that wearing the hat inside was probably making them bald.

The watch desk was manned by the engine or truck on alternate months. Upon assuming watch duty the incoming watchman was required to make the desk journal entry, "Department property examined and found in good order." The guys said it was really to affix blame if something went wrong.

Across the street from the firehouse is the Zion Episcopal Church. One day the new minister came to the firehouse to introduce himself. He held the rank of Canon in the Episcopal church. "Hello" he said to the house watchman Brucy Brown. "I am Canon Downs," to which Brucy famously replied, "Hi. I am Howitzer Brown." That story was retold a lot.

Interestingly the men usually did not tie their shoes. The idea was that you could turn out quicker not having to untie before putting on your boots. At the time I thought it was cool. Looking back on it I think that it was more of a macho thing because the turnouts were not all that fast.

The firemen in those days were isolated in the firehouse. There was a department phone without a dial, when you picked up the receiver it was answered by Queens dispatch. Curiously the number on the phone was Virginia 7 5200 extension 70. I assume the phone must have been a hand me down from somewhere else. There was no public phone and this was long before cell phones. In the mid 1950s, the height of the cold war, a civil defense phone was installed at the watch desk. I am not sure of it's purpose, it never rang and the dial was locked so you could not dial out. Firemen being inventive soon figured out that if you picked up the receiver and quickly tapped out a phone number on the knobs that the receiver rested on, you could call out, but to be successful you had to be really fast, accurate and lucky.

The firemen could not leave quarters except for runs or official business which meant that they could not go to the store to get food or snacks. This is where I came to the rescue. I went to the store for many lunch and ice cream runs on my bike. The firemen would gladly tip me for my food runs. At lunch time I would take orders for six or seven sandwiches without a written list. The guys wondered how I could remember all that but I was young and they were my heroes.

The author on right on the side of H & L 164 circa 1950

I would also pick up the daily newspaper. I would pedal to what was known as Klein's candy store on Northern Boulevard, which was a forerunner of 7 Eleven. It was owned by Julius Klein who lived above the store which was common in New York in those days. Julius didn't have a commute, but he was open twelve hours a day seven days a week, so his wife and sons had to help.

MATRONS

Long ago when pensions were very poor the widows of firemen killed in line of duty often became firehouse matrons. The matron at Engine 313 was Mrs. Finn, the wife of Fireman Thomas S. Finn of Engine 65 who was one of eight firemen who died in the line of duty on August 1, 1932 at the Ritz Tower Hotel at 57th Street and Park Avenue. The fire was in the sub- basement and an explosion occurred. Fireman Finn was killed instantly. The matron was an honorary title, with real duties, and a salary paid by firemen, who imposed a weekly tax on themselves to help the widows of colleagues who died on duty.

In 1932, when Mrs Finn became a fire matron, her fire department pension was $50.00 a month. Her matron job was like a housekeeper, she made the beds and did the tidying up. I remember Mrs. Finn as a quiet older lady who came on weekday mornings and worked upstairs for a few hours. Her comings and goings were recorded in the company desk journal. I believe that the last matrons worked through the 1960s.

THE COMMISSIONER

In 1954, Edward Cavanagh became the Fire Commissioner. He lived in Glen Cove and his car and aide were put up at Engine 313. I would see him sometimes, he seemed to be a friendly man. It was interesting to have his aides there nights and weekends. They knew all the inside dope citywide of what had happened, what was happening and was going to happen.

Cavanagh chose four aides to cover all the shifts. They were a Catholic, a Protestant, a Jew and a Black. I thought that it was neat and fair to try to be inclusive and be everybody's commissioner. He was certainly way ahead of his time in being politically correct. The black fireman was fully accepted as a brother firefighter and race was never an issue. You sometimes hear about racism in society and the department, but it was not the case in the 1950s in the Douglaston firehouse.

AUXILIARIES

During World War 2 the FDNY started an auxiliary program whereby volunteer civilians were organized and trained to supplement the FDNY in wartime in order to be prepared for attacks such as the London blitz. The volunteer turnout to protect the city was huge, around 30,000 volunteered in New York City.

The auxiliaries attended drills, were issued turnout gear and were assigned tours of duty. Those physically fit were permitted to respond to fires. A rank structure was established based on abilities. The auxiliaries were used at almost every major fire during the war years.

My dad was an auxiliary fireman during World War 2. He served at Ladder 36 in upper Manhattan and later at Engine 313 in Douglaston, so we knew many of the same firemen. The auxiliary's continued after the war and I became one when I came of age.

The FDNY auxiliary helmet worn by my father

FIREMAN STICK TOGETHER TO LIVE
By Dennis Hevesi
From an article in Newsday, July 17, 1977

Douglaston - The kitchen door slams. A plate clatters. Abandoned coffee steams in cups on the table. Half a sentence hangs . . . Engines growl, then roar out of the truck bay. In fewer than 30 seconds, the men of Engine Co. 313 and Hook and Ladder 164 are gone, leaving only the wail of sirens fading along 244th Street.

The winding, hilly streets of Douglaston, Bayside and Little Neck, lined with private homes and apartments and a handful of high-rises, do not know the sounds of sirens too intimately. Engine Co. 313 responded to only 907 calls in 1976. Engine Co. 45 in the South Bronx answered 7,829 calls last year. But fire knows nothing of geography. It just burns. The call from box 6403, comes in at 7:56 AM Thursday, little more than an hour before the men of the night tour are about to knock off.

Lt. James Zeppernick, 47, of Wantagh, a veteran of 24 years with the department, is the officer on Engine 313, a 15-ton pumper capable of throwing 1,000 gallons a minute. The fire is on the sixth floor of the building at 54-44 Little Neck Pkwy. It is large enough for a second alarm.

Zeppernick calls for eight lengths of hose, moves into the lobby and up the stairs. Armed only with flashlight and ax, his job is to find the fire. Next to him, at the nozzle, is Frank Gregor, 43, of Mount Sinai. Smoke is seeping from the door of apartment 6M. By now, the irons man from Hook and Ladder I64, carrying an ax and heavy crowbar, has arrived. They force the door, call through their walkie-talkie for water and begin to crawl along the floor.

The smoke tears at their eyes and throats opening their sinuses and spilling the mucous on their chins. The backup man, wearing an airpack arrives with masks. The canned air helps, but Zeppernick and Gregor have already taken a lot of smoke. The fire is in the bedroom. Zeppernick and Gregor do not know it, but the outside ventilation men, whose job it is to break out the windows so the fire can vent to the outside have not been able to get close enough. Zeppernick and Gregor and the backup man crawl to the bedroom door and force it open. The fire smoldering with anticipation bolts for the door and slams the men into semiconsciousness.

Slowly the backup man shakes the mist from his brain. He screams into his walkie-talkie: "Two men down. Two men down." The rescuers come, drag Zeppernick and Gregor to safety, pump oxygen into their lungs. They are lucky this time, just smoke inhalation and heat exposure. They will be back for their regular shifts at the firehouse on 244th Street in a few days.

In reality, there is nothing regular about the shifts. City firemen work two 9-hour day tours in a row, are off for 48 hours, then work two 15 hour night tours in a row. "It's the nature of the job," said Phil Proetto, 44, of Farmingdale, who was working a day tour one day last week. But the schedule takes its toll. There are toe-to-toe beds on the second floor of the firehouse, each with a red, white and blue striped pillow. "We are allowed to sleep at night," Proelto said, "but every time the bell rings it jolts your heart." Even in their sleep, firemen count the bells. "You do pick them up. You're never really out. If it seems like your going, you sit up in bed. You go from sleeping to a full run. Now, you're forcing a door, stretching a hose line, climbing a ladder," Proetto said, "That's where all the heart attacks come from."

Most of the 54 men assigned to Engine Co. 313 and Hook and Ladder 164 are over 40 years old. Two of them, Mike Falabella of Albertson and Hank Kovalesky, who lives three blocks from the firehouse are 56. "I walk to work, Its very convenient," said Kovalesky, who has been with the department for 25 years.

"Most of us put a lot of time in the busy companies" said Stan Corselli, 50, of Bellmore. "I came from Bedford-Stuyvesant. I was down there 16 years. Phil Proetto came from the South Bronx." Proetto said, "I was there 13 years. I have nothing but good memories."

The firemen sometimes watch TV when they aren't answering calls and don't have chores to do around the firehouse. Time between drills and firehouse maintenance, is spent telling "war" stories, and they are not always about fires fought in the old days. "About a month and a half ago," Proetto said, "we were in a private dwelling off Northern Boulevard and we started a line in up to the second floor. The fire met us at the top of the stairs. We moved into a room that was burning. We knocked down the fire, except what seemed to be a pocket. We didn't know it, but it was burning underneath us. We shut down on one side and it came up behind us." I screamed, "Lou, the fire is under us, I was crawling, luckily we got out OK".

"You can't stand up or you get your ears cooked," said Frank Lonigro, 44, of Smithtown. Lonigro is a lieutenant, which is why he is called "Lou." "Remember, in the police department, the officers are out on the street," Proetto said. "With us, it's together." It is the duty of fire lieutenants to go into a building and direct the fight from the site of the fire.

"We eat together, We play together. We sleep together," Proetto said. The firehouse is very much a home away from home. In the morning, after roll call, there is housecleaning. Upstairs, the sheets on the beds are stripped, then laundered. The brass pole (yes, there is one and some of the men use it) is polished. Floors are dusted and mopped.

Lives depend on how well some of the chores are performed. Air packs are checked to make sure the tanks are full. Tools, are cleaned and sharpened. The trucks are refueled; oil levels are checked. They check the 450-gallon tank on the pumper, which provides an immediate supply of water at a fire before the hoses are hooked to hydrants. Hoses are folded, they must not tangle when needed. The trucks are washed and polished. Each fireman folds his running coat on his spot on the truck, sets his helmet on the coat and stands his boots nearby.

Toward noon, whoever has volunteered to cook starts preparing lunch. "We don't mess around" said Bob Burns, 44, of St. James. "Chicken cordon bleu, flounder stuffed with shrimp, we go first class." The men pay and shop for their own food. In order to stay ready for a fire call, all the men drive to the supermarket together on the truck, wearing their gear. One man stays on the truck in radio contact with dispatch. Occasionally, supermarket managers have been left staring at full, but abandoned, shopping carts. Alarm bells seem to ring with irony. "Seems like they go off a lot of times when we're just sitting down to eat" Burns said.

Between them, Engine 313 and Hook and Ladder 164 average only three calls a day. But what appears to be leisure time is punctuated by the dozens of times day and night when the bells rap out a series of numbers or the squawk box informs the companies of messages. Calls for all the units in Queens are heard in each of the firehouses. Each time, there is a tense, frozen moment. Then, the card game defrosts, eyes turn back to the TV set, heads sink back into pillows. There is no pattern, however. There may be no runs for two days or 11 runs in one night.

Engine 313 drilling in front of quarters

It is a tough and dangerous job, but there are those precious moments that make it all worth while. "You pull a baby out and start cardiac massage" Proetto said. "and you see the eyes flutter, My God, he's alive. He is alive."

THE FIREHOUSE

Engine Co. 313 and Hook and Ladder 164 are headquartered in a red-brick, two-story firehouse at 44-01 244th St., one block north of Northern Boulevard in Douglaston. The two units are members of the 53rd Battalion, which covers an area *of northeast Queens generally bounded by the Grand Central Parkway on the south, Francis Lewis Boulevard on the west, the Nassau line on the east and the Queens shoreline on the north. There are five engine companies and three hook and ladder units in the battalion. Engine 313 answered 907 calls in 1976, 717 of which were fires. Hook and Ladder 164, answered 1223 calls, 601 of which were fires.*

CHAPTER 10

THE F.D.N.Y. IN THE 1950s

The following articles are reprinted from WNYF magazine with permission to give the reader a flavor for the culture in the FDNY that Engine 313 and Ladder 164 were a part of in the 1950s.

WNYF stands for "With New York Firemen," and is the FDNY official magazine that dates back to the first issue in 1941. I subscribed to the magazine in 1950 and I may hold a record for the longest subscription. Anyone can subscribe, just google WNYF for a subscription. Many of the 1938 hires started to retire during 1958 and some of them gave me their collection of back issues, so I have an almost complete collection.

In that era WNYF was less technical and more human interest. It published short stories, poems and cartoons, which were submitted by the firemen themselves. WNYF solicited firemen to have their articles published in WNYF, as shown in the "Firemanecdotes" shown below.

The following are true short stories submitted by firemen

THE POLE'S ORIGIN

One version of the origin of poles dates back to 1870, when John J. Bresnan was captain of Engine 13. Fireman Daniel Lawler, cabinet maker by trade, cut a hole in the bunkroom floor and installed a wooden pole. When the captain accused him of disfiguring the building, the fireman proved its advantages over the stairway. Lawler served 50 years before retiring as captain of H. & L. 14.

John J. Bresnan, Jr.,
Chief Dispatcher, Bronx.

THE IRISH BOX

LOOK UP THE location of Manhattan Box 301. It's a description of a little bit of Ireland: Green(e) and Grand.

Timothy W. McVeety, Lieut., H. 4.

ON A POSTAL CARD

We've all heard of the expression when a remote box taps in that "we wouldn't go on a postal card." Well here is the exception that proves the rule. On June 30, 1940, at 12:52 P. M., a small girl, about 8 years of age, came rushing into quarters and handed the man on watch a penny postal. The house-

watchman, thinking perhaps it was some trifling 'ad,' dropped by the letter-carrier, was about to file it with the rest of the mail at the side of the desk. One look, however, at the message scrawled across the front of the card, and the fireman hit the still button. The message read, "Please come to Apartment 6-B, 486 East 165th Street My house is on fire." The officer tapped out both companies, 5-7-2541, and we rolled out to a two hour worker on the top floor.

Joseph T. Lienhard
Fireman, Engine 50

FLOOR PLEASE

Several years ago, a first alarm assignment responded to a call in mid-Manhattan. The fire was in an old-fashioned hotel and apparently on the  first floor. The first due engine crew stretched a handline into the lobby to find an antiquated e l e - vator car — you k n o w , o n e of those beautifully panelled jobs, going mad. The line was opened and directed on the blazing interior when, suddenly, the car started up the shaft. The company had to dash up the stairs with rolled-up lengths and finish the job—on the top floor.

Andrew X. Quinn,
Captain, Engine 14.

(With Apologies to Shakespeare)

POEMS BY FIREMEN

True love

Last night I held a lovely hand,
A hand so soft and neat,
I thought my heart would burst with Joy,
So wildly did it beat.
No other hand unto my heart,
Could greater solace bring,
Than the dear hand I held last night,
Four aces and a king.

Submitted by Emil A. Nemeth, Fireman Engine 54

On The 6x9

At six p.m. when the taps come in,
Our fifteen hours of duty begin.
The roll is called and we check our masks,
And, then we start our routine tasks.
The man on watch takes in the flag,
The messenger drops off the bag.
Two men in the kitchen, (our hamburger cooks)
The students now deeply engrossed in their books.
The rig is wiped down, and the fire's alright,
Oh! and doesn't the garbage go out tonight.
The phone at the watch gives three loud rings,
All hark to the location, the house watch sings.
Quick, turn off the stove, this meal won't be done,
Till the fire's put out and we're back from this run.

Fr. Charles R. Crawford,
Chiefs Aide. 1st Division

You must be the new kid on the job

"I don't care about the parking situation—put it back!"

"This is Chief Klotz. Hope you haven't changed your clothes yet, Lieut.—here's a last minute detail to the other side of the Division."

THE SEAGULL OR BUZZARD
There's one in every house—eats everything
and anything, provided it's for free.

Engine 313 - Hook & Ladder 164

Engine 306 - Hook & Ladder 152 - BC 53

The firehouses in the 53rd Battalion in 1956

Engine 320 - Hook & Ladder 167

Engine/Quad 251

In the 1950s Fireman Jim Martin of Engine 8 resigned to become a priest. It was a hugely big deal for many of his brother firefighters. His career as a priest was reported and posted and watched regularly throughout the department and he was made an honorary chaplain.

FIREMAN JIM NOW FATHER MARTIN

Photo courtesy of WNYF

In July 1958, Engineer of Steamer Otto Kutke retired after a 45 year career, his retirement made that rank nonexistent; he was the last of the engineers who operated the coal burning steam pumpers.

An Engineer of Steamer badge
Photo courtesy of WNYF

RUNS AND WORKERS FOR 1956

ENGINE COMPANIES			LADDER COMPANIES		
No.	Co.	Runs	No.	Co.	Runs
1	53	2135	1	26	2045
2	91	1872	2	43	1591
3	60	1667	3	40	1490
4	35	1536	4	103	1422
5	82	1513	5	120	1360
6	233	1400	6	103	1313
7	59	1462	7	102	1302
8	73	1455	8	110	1298
9	80	1304	9	18	1263
10	290	1293	10	123	1256
11	50	1233	11	31	1284
12	17	1299	12	105	1244
13	37	1258	13	30	1243
14	36	1250	14	111	1230
15.	231	1246	15	28	1231
16	54	1243	16	47	1211
17	94	1333	17	19	1210
18	41	1311	18	14	1171
19	47	1185	19	42	1163
20	76	1083	20	22	1136

NOTABLE FDNY EVENTS IN THE 1950s

The FDNY band was disbanded (pun not intended) in 1958.

During the 1950s there was a shift from wood aerials and ground ladders to metal.

In October 1956 ladder pipes were installed on 26 aerial trucks, giving the department 26 new water towers.

Thirty-three new chiefs cars came equipped with seat belts in October 1956.

The FDNY Emerald Society was founded in1956.

In July 1956 air horns were tested and showed that the new horn is much more effective than the conventional siren.

Life in 1956

President: Dwight D. Eisenhower

Average income: $4,454

World Series champions, the New York Yankees, 4-3 over the Brooklyn Dodgers

Elvis Presley emerges as one of the world's first rock stars

Prices: Average FDNY firemen's salary $5,000

Average House: $22,000

Average car: $2,500

Reingold Beer 6-pack $1.20

CHAPTER 11

COMMENDATIONS AND AWARDS

A company may be eligible for a unit citation if they show initiative and/or bravery that is beyond its normal function. For example an engine company is expected to put out a fire. If however they also rescue victims while extinguishing a fire a detailed report is made out by the officer in command of the company.

The chief in charge of the operation investigates and makes a recommendation. If he determines that the act is worthy of recognition, it is forwarded to the Board of Merit.

The Board of Merit is composed of experienced and respected officers, who decide the award, based on the facts presented. Engine 313 was awarded the commendations shown below for outstanding service at a house fire at 123 Warwick Avenue in Douglaston Manor, and for the actions of Engine 313 and Ladder 164 at a 3rd alarm fire involving eight attached frame buildings under construction. See the article about this fire in the Runs and Workers chapter.

FIRE DEPARTMENT CITY OF NEW YORK AWARDS

CLASS A

Engine Company 313

Date of Act	Box#	Address
Monday, July 04, 1983	75-6349	123 Warwick Avenue
Tuesday, September 11, 1979	33-3935	240-15 thru 240-25 70th Avenue

Ladder Company 164

Date of Act	Box#	Address
Tuesday, September 11, 1979	33-3935	240-15 thru 240-25 70th Avenue

A heroic rescue by Captain Stanzoni, Engine 313

Captain Gary Stanzoni, Engine 313
FDNY photo

On Saturday August 4, 2007, the Queens dispatch office received a phone call at 1427 hours, reporting a house fire with people trapped at 218-05 36th Avenue in the Bayside section of Queens. When the call was sent out, Engine 313 housed in Douglaston and under the command of Captain Gary E. Stanzoni - was the second-due engine on the dispatch ticket. On arrival Engine 306 transmitted the 10-75 for a working fire in a two-story 20 by 40 foot private dwelling.

When Engine 313 arrived at the job, the members assisted Engine 306 stretching the first hose line. Before the first truck company arrived, Captain Stanzoni was met in front of the house by a woman who was screaming that her mother was trapped in the rear of the burning house. Without hesitation, Captain Stanzoni entered the front door of the house and quickly ascended the stairs to the second floor that was on fire. At the top of the stairs Captain Stanzoni was confronted with high heat, heavy black smoke and zero visibility. The fire originated in the bedroom in the front of the house and extended into the hallway, leading to the bathroom and other bedrooms.

At this time, the first hose-line was being stretched and was not yet in operation. Without the protection of an operating hose-line Captain Stanzoni went past the main body of fire to the rear of the house and found an unconscious woman Dorothy Cahn, in the rear bathroom.

He proceeded to carry Ms. Cahn past the fire, down the stairs and out to the front lawn, where it was determined that she was unconscious, but still breathing. Ms.

Cahn was turned over to EMS personnel and transported to the North Shore Hospital. Despite the heroic efforts of Captain Stanzoni, Ms. Cahn passed away as a result of her injuries.

For his actions in trying to save the life of Dorothy Cahn, the FDNY officially recognized Captain Gary E. Stanzoni of Engine 313 and presented him with the Ner Tamid Society/Franklin Delano Roosevelt Medal.

The following are letters of thanks from people who were helped by the members of Engine 313 and Ladder 164:

On April 21, 1992, my neighbors home had a serious fire. The members of your Department who responded from Engines 326, 304, 301, and 251, and Ladders I60, and 164, were to say the least superb. In what seemed like minutes the fire was out without it spreading throughout the structure or to other houses. All members present at this fire should be commended for doing a job over and beyond the call of duty.

Take care and God bless.

Edward Pearce. EMT Queens Village

Lieutenant Willaim Wira
Engine Co. 313
Queens, N.Y.

Dear Lieutenant Wira

On July 3rd my husband was stricken with a heart attack and a call for help was made to the Fire Department.

Your Engine Company 313 responded to this call. You and your men were absolutely wonderful and my heartfelt thanks goes to each and every one of you.

Your immediate and life saving response averted what would have been a most tragic and sorrowful experience.

My husband is now recuperating at North Shore Hospital and doing well as a result of your great men. My prayers and love will be with you firemen always.

Gratefully, Cecelia McCarton
33-16 255 Street
Little Neck, NY

CHAPTER 12

FIREFIGHTER DEATHS

The time was 8:04 A.M., July 2nd, 1950. The bells at Engine 313 sounded box 6150, Northern Boulevard and the Alley Creek Bridge, both companies first due. Captain Thomas F. Munroe of Engine 313 collapsed when responding to the apparatus floor. At Flushing Hospital Captain Munroe was diagnosed as having had a coronary thrombosis. He was later assigned to the Limited Service Squad and retired with a disability retirement. He suffered another heart attack several years later that was fatal. He was 65 years old. His death was ruled a line of duty death.

Engine 313's journal entry detailing the response to box 6150 and documenting Captain Munroe collapsing upon the apparatus floor reads as follows:

7:52 A.M. Received alarm by telegraph signal 6150 both companies responded.

8:04 A.M. Engine 313 and H&L I64 returned to quarters from station 6150 in service signal 4-4-4 - 313 and 4-4-4 - 7 - 164 transmitted and received 2-3 in reply. False Alarm. Box rewound and reset. Dispatcher notified.

Upon return to quarters Lieutenant Bailey HL164 records that upon receipt of above signal 6150 Captain Munroe Engine 313 collapsed upon response to the apparatus floor. Ordered Fr. Myhrburg Eng 313 to take him to the nearest doctor. Upon return Fr Myhrburg informed me that Dr. McGinley had ordered him to Flushing hospital. Notified Batt Chief Sneeden, Deputy Chief 14th Division, Dispatcher #14, Deputy Chief of Staff and Operations, also the Medical Officer Dr. Rosenfeld through the dispatcher.

I was a kid at the time and remembered Captain Munroe well, he was always nice to me. At the time of his heart attack my friend Frank and I picked wild flowers for him and delivered them to the firehouse. At the firehouse they told us to deliver them to Captain Munroe's home which was in the neighborhood. Little did I know that fifty years later I would be honored to deliver his eulogy at the dedication of his line of duty death plaque at Engine 313. The plaque was probably delayed because his heart attack did not immediately result in his death. I was invited to the dedication ceremony as I was the only person that they could find who actually knew the captain.

The desk journal entry documenting Captain Munroe's collapse

The department order announcing the death of Captain Munroe

FIRE DEPARTMENT

CITY OF NEW YORK

UNIFORMED FORCE

DEPARTMENT
ORDER NO. 39   February 28, 1968

1.1   With regret, the death of retired Captain *Thomas F. Munroe*, L.S.S., Fire Emergency Division (Engine Co. 313), residing at 45-27 243rd Street, Douglaston, Queens, N. Y., which occurred on February 26, 1968, is hereby announced to the department.

Funeral will.take place from the Leo F. Kearns Funeral Home, 61-40 Woodhaven Boulevard, Rego Park. Queens, N. Y., on March 2, 1968, followed by a Requiem Mass at 0945 hrs., at St. Anastasia R. C. Church, 45-14 245th Street, Douglaston, Queens. N. Y. Interment at Calvary Cemetery.

The viewing hours at the funeral home will be from 1900 hrs. to 2200 hrs., February 28, 1968 and from 1000 hrs. to 2200 hrs. commencing February 29, 1968.

The deputy chief of the 16th Division shall detail one lieutenant and six firemen as Funeral Escort. Escort shall report in front of the above-named Church at 0915 hrs., March 2, 1968. After services they shall accompany the remains a reasonable distance when escort shall be dismissed.

The plaque honoring Captain Munroe
Photo by Jimmy Raftery FDNY Dispatcher

Captain Thomas F. Munroe

LIEUTENANT ORESTES HANTJILES

Lieutenant Hantjiles, Engine 313 died on November 28th, 1959 from a fire at the Brinkhoff's Inn located at 220th Street and Northern Boulevard in Bayside. I was unaware of the fire and happened upon it. The first thing I saw was Rescue 4 from Woodside in the street. It was a bad sign, I had never seen the rescue in the 53rd battalion before.

When I arrived the fire was out and overhaul was in progress. I talked to a few of the guys and they told me that Lieutenant Hantjiles collapsed had been transported to the hospital. It seemed to be routine and no one was concerned. I continued on my way and stopped at 313.

The fire commissioners aide was in quarters since it was a Saturday, and he told me that Lieutenant Hantjiles had died. I was shocked and returned to the fireground and notified E313 & L164. "Who told you that?" they replied skeptically. I told them that the fire commissioners aide told me. Everyone was shocked. Later I was in the firehouse when they returned from the fire. No one could believe what had happened. Later, one of the firemen unthinking said "whose shoes are those sitting on the apparatus floor." I can still see those shoes. He was a nice quiet man who had transferred in a few years before from the Bronx. Lieut. Hantjiles was only 43 years old.

Orestes Hantjiles
Lieutenant
Engine Co. 313

The following quote is from the Long Island Star Journal:

"Responding to a restaurant fire, Lt. Hantjiles entered a three story building at 219-20 Northern Boulevard, Bayside. He never came out alive. Aged 43, he leaves behind a wife, and no children. The funeral was held from Leo F. Kearns Funeral Home in Rego Park last Monday."

The Fire Department order that announced the line of duty death of Lieutenant Hantjiles reads "With regret, the death of Lieutenant Orestes Hantjiles, Engine Co. 313 which occurred on November 28, 1959, as a result of Injuries sustained at Box 6995, Queens, is hereby announced to the department."

FIREMAN DIES IN QUEENS

Lieutenant Collapses During Blaze in Restaurant

A 43-year-old fire lieutenant collapsed while fighting a fire in a restaurant building at 219-20 Northern Boulevard, Bayside, Queens, yesterday, and died a few minutes later.

The police said Lieut. Orestes Hantjiles of 82-27 249th Street, Bellerose, Queens, had entered the burning three-story building wearing an oxygen mask. He was in Engine Company 313. The Fire Department said smoke inhalation or a heart attack could have caused his death. An autopsy will be performed.

There was heavy damage to the building. The cause of the fire was not known.

Orestes Hantjiles
Lieutenant
Engine Co. 313

Died on November 28, 1959, as a result of injuries sustained in the performance of duty at Box 6995, Queens. Appointed July 1, 1941 and assigned to Engine Co. 273.

Fireman Dies; Upper Floor Razed In Fire Saturday At Brinkhoff's

FIREMEN BATTLE upper floor blaze Saturday morning at Brinkhoff's Inn at Northern Boulevard and 220th Street. Lower right, Long Island Jewish Hospital ambulance arrives to give emergency treatment to Lt. Orestes Hantjlles who was fatally stricken while leading his men in fighting the fire.

AN ARTICLE FROM THE BAYSIDE TIMES, NOVEMBER 30TH, 1959

*A fireman died Saturday morning while fighting an upper-story
blaze at Brinkhoff's Inn, Northern Boulevard and 220th Street
in Bayside. Lt. Orestes Hantjiles of Engine Company 313
was leading his men in fighting the fire when he was fatally
stricken. The 43 year old fire department officer who was
eligible for retirement in about one year, was rushed to
Long Island Jewish Hospital by ambulance but was declared
dead-on-arrival at the Glen Oaks Hospital.*

*He was wearing an oxygen inhalator when he entered the
building, and the Fire Department said a heart attack or
smoke poisoning could have caused his death. Autopsy
will determine the exact cause.*

*According to the department, the fire caused "heavy" damage.
John Brinkhoff, owner of the popular Bayside nightspot, said
that damage was restricted to the upper story of the three-floor
structure. Cause is still unknown.*

*He told the Bayside Times that he will be able to reopen as
soon as roofing can be built to cover the gaping hole in the
third story. He said that there was no damage to the lower
floors. All heating, gas and electricity is in working order he added.*

*The fire was reported at 11:30 A.M. and Engine Company 313,
stationed at 44-01 244th Street, Douglaston, raced to the scene.
Lt. Hantjiles was stricken shortly after noon.*

*Police blocked off Northern Boulevard to all traffic, until the blaze
was brought under control.*

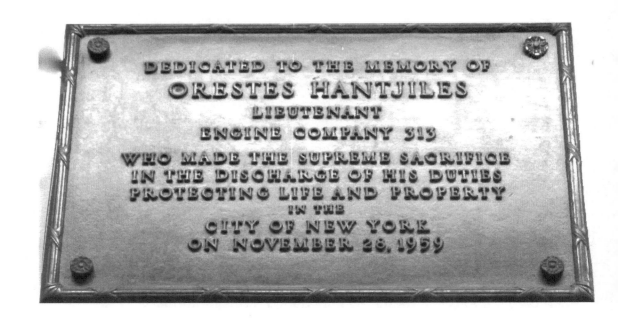

The plaque honoring Lieutenant Hantjiles
Photo by Jimmy Raftery FDNY Dispatcher

The plaque dedications for both Captain Munroe and Lieutenant Hantjiles were held in quarters on October 10th, 2007 which was Firemen's Memorial Day. The dedication also included a rededication of the plaque for Lieutenant Orestes Hantjiles Engine 313 which was moved into a more prominent position alongside Captain Munroe. Following the ceremony I went on the bus carrying the members of Engine 3l3 and Tower Ladder l64 to the FDNY Memorial Day remembrance held annually in Manhattan at the Firemen's Monument on Riverside Drive.

The Firemen's Monument honors the FDNY members who died in the line of duty. It was very impressive and moving. Over 5,000 FDNY firefighters marched and I was honored to be there. Afterwards we all went on to some division coalitions which are celebrations held at halls and restaurants where food and drink are served, providing a nice ending. Following the ceremony a group picture was taken of the officers and members of Engine 313 and Tower Ladder 164. The author is shown with the light colored pants.

FDNY
Engine 313 Ladder 164

LIEUTENANT THOMAS HODGES ENGINE 313

Lieutenant Thomas Hodges of Engine 313 died due to a World Trade Center related illness from repeated exposure to WTC toxins which has caused many cancers, respiratory and lung problems. Over 50 other firefighters have died in the years since 9/11/2001 from illnesses contracted during prolonged operations at the World Trade Center. Everyone is aware of the horrendous losses suffered by the FDNY on 9/11, but few realize that the firefighter death toll continues to rise.

ENGINE 313 & LADDER 164 DEATHS FROM NATURAL CAUSES 1957

Lieutenant William J. Bailey, Hook & Ladder 164 died of natural causes at 4 P.M. February 22nd, 1957. He was appointed on June 16, 1929.

Fireman Frederick Coppers, Engine 313 died on April 3rd, 1957 at 3:30 A.M. however Fireman Zwerle apparently edited the time of death in the desk journal to 3:13 A.M. Fred was appointed to the department on June 1st, 1917.

Captain Charles W. Heintz of Ladder 164 died at 12:30 P.M. on August 5th, 1957 at his home in Little Neck of natural causes.

During 1957 the signal 5-5-5-5 indicating the death of a member was transmitted 19 times. Three were for line of duty deaths and sixteen for the natural death of an active member. Line of duty deaths have declined dramatically and currently there is an average of about five natural deaths of active members annually. This reflects the improved fireground safety practices and better monitoring of members health.

CHAPTER 13

COMMUNICATIONS

As a kid I remember running down to Northern Boulevard when I heard both companies running toward Little Neck. The Bayside companies, Engine 306, Ladder 152 and Battalion 53 always responded past because there were no apparatus radios. (At that time all these units were with E306 in Bayside).

Radios were installed in Engine 313 and Ladder 164 in 1952, I was there the day that they were installed. With the radio all responding units could hear the street address, and companies could be returned before their arrival, or they could be redirected. Before the radio, communications with Queens dispatch from the street was by using the telegraph key inside the fire boxes.

Before radios, companies would usually respond back to quarters (at a reduced speed) because they were out of service until they were in quarters. The practice of responding back continued for quite awhile after radios were installed, change came slowly.

THE BELL SYSTEM

Fire companies were dispatched by telephone and telegraph. The first due engine and truck would get a phone call from the Queens dispatch. At first, fire calls were an ordinary ring, later fire calls were three sharp rings on the phone. Units other than first due just got the telegraph signal to respond to the closest box location and they would pick up the address on the air while responding.

In the days before the 911 system, you would dial the operator to report a fire, who would connect you to the fire department. The alarm as today was dispatched as a phone alarm.

When a phone alarm was received in the firehouse, the watchman would write down the address of the alarm in chalk on the blackboard, and holler "Get Out" which would be repeated throughout the house, and then he would hit the still button which would manually ring the bells in the house and push the master switch which turned on all the lights. There was no verification to Queens dispatch that the units were responding.

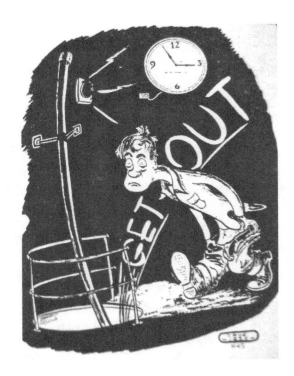

On the wall behind the watch desk was a 1929 hand drawn map of Douglaston showing the streets and the box locations.

A pulled street box came into Queens dispatch with four rounds of the box number. Dispatch then transmitted the box to the companies.

The watch desk had two large bells on an electrical panel, one was the primary circuit and the other the secondary, (a backup). Signals would come in twice, first on the primary, then repeated on the secondary. Each bell had a slightly different tone. Small repeater bells were in the sitting room, bunk room and officers rooms.

When an alarm came in by telegraph, the box number would go on the blackboard and the housewatch would look up the box number in the assignment cards which were located at the watch desk. These cards showed all the boxes that the companies would respond to. If the companies were due to respond he would turn out the company. If the card showed a response on the second alarm, he would call out for example, "Bell Boulevard and 41st Avenue, first due on the second." If it was a distant box with no card, he may call out "We go on the postcard," meaning that it was so far away, that if they should need us they would write us a letter. Firehouse humor.

6315	RUSHMORE AVENUE & 245TH STREET								QUEENS
									DOUGLASTON

ENGINE CO'S	BOAT	RES CO.	H & L CO'S	D.C.	C OF B	SPCL	GOW	RESV CHIEF	COMPANIES TO CHANGE LOCATION	
									ENGINE CO'S	H. & L. Co's
313 306			164 152		53			52		
320 274 273 272			167	14				13	304 - 313 296 - 320 324 - 273	150 - 152
295 301 315		4	129		54		13		298 - 304 287 - 295 303 - 301	138 - 129
317 275 299									314 - 317	
289 316 305 319									270 - 299 293 - 305 325 - 289	

A 1950s Douglaston assignment card
Cards provided courtesy of "G" - Man, Tom Eve

The assignment card above shows all the companies due to respond or relocate up through a fifth alarm. The GOW column was for the gas and oil wagon, SPCL is for special units, reserve chiefs are those who would be special called if the assigned chief was unavailable. Notice how few truck companies and chiefs were assigned, and that the rescue didn't respond until the third alarm. One advantage of this bell and card system was that it was fast and provided automatic relocations.

When a box assignment was short the dispatcher only had to dispatch one engine, one truck and a battalion chief. Units responding had no knowledge of what, if any units other than the minimum would be responding.

A signal 7-5 (all hands working) was transmitted to all Queens companies and companies due on the second alarm turned out on the apparatus floor prepared to respond if a second alarm was transmitted. During 1956, E313/LI64 turned out for four of these 7-5 signals, none of which became second alarms.

Class 3: This was the preliminary signal for an **automatic fire alarm** from a central station monitoring company or building box. It would be dispatched as a telegraph signal such as 3 - 6340 - 1. The assignment card for the box would show the location of the building. The number 1 was referred to as the terminal which indicated where the alarm came from within the building. For example terminal 1 could be the alarm was from the basement, terminal 2 could be the furnace room etc.

The box numbers in the Douglaston, Little Neck area were mostly in the 6300 & 6400 series as they are today. The numbers came in very rapidly, you couldn't accurately count them if you weren't used to it. All incoming signals were recorded in the desk journal using pen and ink.

A Douglaston Street Box

Engine 313 responded to all the boxes in the 6300 series, and most of the 6400 series. It was unusual for companies to respond to all the boxes in a series and to be first due at all of them. This meant that if the bells started with 63 you knew that you were going on a first due run, which speeded up the companies turning out. That changed in the late 1950s when some of the 6300 series numbers that were not used were moved elsewhere in Queens. The reaction of the firemen was interesting. Some of the firemen didn't care, they said no problem just count the bells. Many (including me) were upset, it was messing with "our boxes" and tradition.

In Douglaston about 2/3 of the alarms received were by both telephone and telegraph. The remaining l/3 were by telegraph only meaning it was a pull box with no phone call. Most pull boxes were for brush fires, and about 15% were false alarms. At boxes where nothing was evident, members would fan out to scour the area for fire.

At Engine 313 there was sometimes a problem with the receipt of telegraph alarms, because you could hear rapid clicks as the box was sending its number to Queens.

Then when Queens sent the box number to the companies, it came in messed up, a combination of bells and clicks, which usually required a phone call to straighten out.

Queens Fire Dispatch 1955
Photo courtesy of WNYF

One day we heard the clicks from a pulled box come in very slowly 6-4-0-0, and the second round started 6-4 and then stopped. When Queens dispatch did not transmit the box, the house watchman called dispatch who did not get the signal. The box was transmitted and it turned out to be a minor house fire.

Normally boxes were transmitted to certain areas, for example Engine 313 would get all alarms in the 53rd and 52nd battalions which was from Flushing to the city line and east to Hillside Ave. However when things got busy, you would get the entire borough. All multiple alarms in the city went out on the bells to all companies.

Usually the bells were infrequent, but at times particularly during the brush fire season it could get really busy. On one of those busy days I was helping the watchman by recording the alarms on the blackboard, while the watchman was entering them in the desk journal. When it got this busy it was easy to stop paying attention to the bells. Suddenly 6334 came in both companies first due, nobody was reacting so I told the watchman who turned the companies out. Upon arriving the lieutenant opened the box and said, "this box was not pulled." He looked at the house watchman, who then looked at me, my heart sunk. Then the lieutenant said, "Wait, it was pulled." A big sigh of relief. The alarm was false.

On another very busy day there was a huge brush fire in Queens and a few of the firemen were at the watch desk listening to engine after engine being dispatched to the fire. One of the firemen had the bright idea for a joke to use the still button to ring the bells to replicate a dispatch for Engine 313 to respond. It started out all right but he soon messed up and made the bell sound like a run had come in by phone, which turned out the house expecting a run. Lieutenant Comiskey slid the pole and was steaming mad that anyone would fool with the bells. Needless to say that never happened again.

I once pulled box 6997 Northern Boulevard and 223rd Street for a large brush fire in the area that was known as the meadows. I was surprised by the loud mechanical and electrical noise it made as it was transmitting.

During the 1930s and 1940s a pulled street box received a full response. If the fire was phoned in, and no street box was pulled, the alarm response was a single engine, truck and chief. The reason that this crazy system existed was because the street boxes had preceded the telephone, and in the early years the telegraph was the primary source of alarms. When the telephone came into general use, the dispatch system didn't quickly adjust to the changes. The dispatch system was also slow to change away from the street boxes as technology, especially cell phones made them obsolete.

The bell system became antiquated and the last bells rang in 1983, but the system had worked well for a century. An example of how well it could work was the simultaneous alarm recorded in Engine 313's desk journal on December 3rd, 1957. The fire was on the Luckenback Pier at the foot of 35th Street in Brooklyn. Companies arrived to find an advanced fire in a one story 175 x 1700 foot pier. After the 5th alarm a major explosion rocked the pier. Dozens of firemen were injured and a fireboat suffered major damage.

The simultaneous call was used after the 5th alarm to bring additional alarms from Manhattan. The signal 77 1499 66 44 36 transmitted in Manhattan caused the 16 engine companies and 6 ladder companies due on the fourth alarm at box 36 in lower Manhattan to respond to the five alarm fire at box 1499 in Brooklyn. The relocating companies relocated automatically.

If a similar signal was transmitted in Queens and the Bronx, 48 engine companies could be sent to Brooklyn's 5th alarm with only three transmissions, one signal in each borough.

The bell system's weakness was when things got really busy the system would bog down. For example if none of the first alarm companies were available, an engine, truck and chief would be special called by the bells. An example of the transmissions may be 5-9450-315, 7-9450-129 and 4-9450-49, and each signal would be sent twice. It is easy to see how the bell system would go nuts during storms and busy times. The same problem existed with the FDNY radio system, during busy times the radio traffic went crazy, so the ten code system was developed to reduce excess radio traffic.

Another disadvantage to the bell system is that when the bells rang you never knew if it was a response for you, most were for other companies, but you had to count the bells to find out. Today when the tones go off you know that it is a response.

Listening to the bells all those years it seemed to get in to my DNA. I have found that to this day when I idly tap my fingers, I sometimes catch myself unconsciously tapping a box number.

There was a telegraph key in the fire boxes and in the pre-radio days it was used for signaling dispatch that the box was false, a working fire or request a multiple alarm. The telegraph key in the firehouse was usually used to notify dispatch that the companies were back In quarters. The watchman would transmit 4-4-4 - 313 and the acknowledgement would come back 2-3. The truck would send 4- 4-4 - 7- 164.

The key was also used to report verbal alarms. Once a verbal alarm was reported to Engine 313 for a serious auto accident on Northern Boulevard. The morse key at the watch desk was used to send the signal 5-7 6336 to Queens.

In 1947, a 2nd, 3rd 4th and 5th alarms were transmitted from the morse key in the quarters of Engine 23 in Manhattan for a fire in the firehouse block.

Some of these old telegraph system signals are used today as part of the ten code. For example a working fire was transmitted as a 7-5 signal. The 5-7 signal heard today originated as the preliminary telegraph signal for an engine company which was 5 and a truck company which was 7. Thus a 5-7 signal would be for the first due engine and truck to respond to a box. The signal 9-2 was used to indicate a false alarm, and the 65-2 was turn on apparatus radios for a department message.

In the 1950s there were not many inter-borough responses citywide. Most Queens assignment cards were all Queens companies all the way up to a fifth alarm as shown previously in the sample assignment card. The exceptions were near the shared Brooklyn border and directly across the river from Manhattan. Today a multiple alarm in Douglaston would have Bronx companies pouring over the bridges.

MUTUAL AID

Mutual aid is either by a request through channels or by responding to an alarm near the city border to a fire that is located outside the city. Previously, mutual aid to surrounding jurisdictions was informal, but in recent years formal mutual aid agreements have been established. In Queens, box 500 was established at the quarters of Engine 313 for mutual aid assistance to adjacent Nassau County. The first alarm mutual aid response is E306, E320, TL164, L167 BC 53. Additional alarms can be transmitted from these mutual aid boxes as needed.

Tower Ladder 164 operating at mutual aid in Nassau
County, Queens box 6398, November 7, 2010
Photo courtesy of WNYF

CHAPTER 14

RUNS AND WORKERS

In 1956 the runs in Douglaston were few and far between. That year the engine had 304 runs, averaging 25 runs a month. The monthly high was 42 runs in April (brush fire season) and a low of 11 runs in October. Ladder 164 had 233 runs averaging 19 runs a month, and ran only 6 times during the year without the engine. In early March 1957, E313 & L164 went for 10 days without a run. The most runs in a 24 hour period was 5, all brush fires.

There was a closet in the firehouse basement that contained all the desk journals from 1929 when the house was established. I looked through them years ago and found that in the 1930s there were months when neither company turned a wheel. Most fire companies were not very busy in that era. In 1940 Engine 91 in Manhattan was the busiest engine company in the city with 1056 runs, and they were the only company to top 1000 runs.

Total alarms during the 1950s were much less frequent than today. In 1955 FDNY responses were 150,00 compared to 450,00 today. While total alarms during the 1950s were much less frequent, there were more multiple alarms, clocking ten fifth alarms and fourteen-fourth alarms in a typical year. This was probably a reflection of the heavier industrial and manufacturing base in the city at that time.

While Engine 313 and Hook & Ladder 164's runs were infrequent, they had some very long runs. During the 1950s, the guys used to talk about the long first due runs that they used to have before Engine 251 was established. They still have the long runs but at least the engine is not first due there anymore.

To give you an idea of the size of E313/TL164's district, the distance from the tip of the of the Douglaston Manor peninsula to the furthest runs on Union Turnpike is a distance of 4.7 miles. In Manhattan, the same distance is from 23rd Street to 110th Street.

There are many reasons why the Engine 313's runs were so few. The area was not fully built up. There were few buildings south of what became the Long Island Expressway, although that changed rapidly. There were no medical calls, almost no automatic fire alarms, no 3rd or 4th due engines, no highway boxes, no CO detectors, FAST trucks, (standby for firefighter rescue) few gas leaks, and no car accidents or relocations. A single engine responded to vehicle fires and the parkways. Neither company ever relocated and they were not assigned anywhere above a second alarm. E313 was always covered by a relocater usually E304 or E274 if they were operating for a prolonged period, or if they responded to a second alarm.

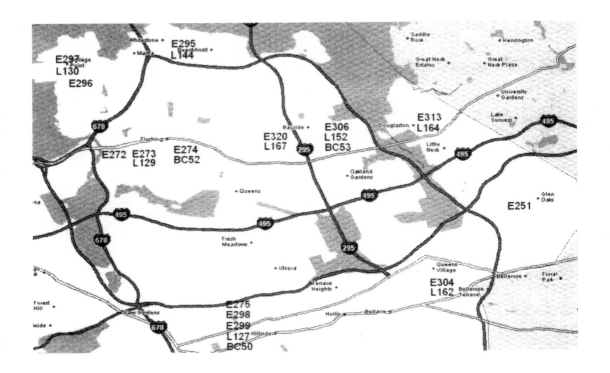

Firehouse locations in northeast Queens in 1955
Map courtesy of Ignatius Kapalczynski

The response assignment cards in most of Queens called for a 2 engines, 2 trucks and one battalion chief (B.C.) response. Multiple phone calls did not increase the response to a 4 engines and 2 truck response as is done today.

A 7-5 signal brought a deputy chief, but no additional units. Back then there were no squads and Rescue 4 was not assigned in the 53rd battalion until the third alarm which almost never happened.

To give you an idea of FDNY activity in northeast Queens in that era, E313 would normally receive all the alarms for companies in the 52nd and 53rd battalions. This consisted of E272 (now disbanded), E273, E274, E295, E296 (now disbanded), E297, E320, E306, E313, E251, L129, L130, L144, L152 (then with E306) and L167.

Engine 313's journals show that about 40% of the time no alarms at all were transmitted between midnight and 6 A.M., which means that none of the 16 companies in either battalion turned a wheel all night, there no all hands fires in Queens or multiple alarms anywhere in the city. Engine 313 turned out 10 times in one year between these hours.

In later years as the runs increased throughout the city, Engine 313's and Ladder 164's runs also increased as shown:

Engine 313		Ladder 164	
1956	304	1956	220
1964	406	1964	600
1970	612	1970	1004
1973	996	1973	1223
2011	1669	2011	1571

Engine 313's average runs through the years compared to all FDNY engines places them at about 190 out of 197 engines in the city. Tower Ladder 164 averages about 128 out of 143 ladder trucks.

Engine 251 was established in 1952, assuming the company number of the disbanded Engine 251 in Brooklyn. After a few years Engine 251 was converted to what was called a quad. There were a half dozen of them in the city and they were very controversial. This was a concept that you could combine an engine and a truck in one company. It looked like an elongated pumper and carried lots of ground ladders and I believe had a seven man crew. The idea was that it would be both an engine and a truck company because of the extra men and equipment assigned. Of course it didn't work very well, and the troops hated it, but it lasted quite a while. I think that in reality they were a heavily staffed engine, not both. Responses were reduced to 2 engines and 1 truck since E251 was considered both an engine and a truck, which reduced Ladder 164's runs. Quad 251 was not assigned on any multiple alarms and never relocated. Engine 251 does not relocate to this day.

The dedication of Engine 251 in 1952
Photo courtesy of WNYF

An FDNY Quad
Photo courtesy of WNYF

FIRES

When I was 15 I rode my bike to a pull box for a car fire on Northern Boulevard in Little Neck. Charlie Rowan asked me "Did you ride with us." A light bulb went off, it never occurred to me that I might be able to respond with the engines.

I started plotting how I could do it. One night my big chance came, box 9781 came in for Springfield Boulevard and Horace Harding Boulevard, a long 2nd due run. I asked Lieutenant Hamilton "Can I go with you." He said yes, so I jumped on the side of the truck. I was scared to death and hung on with a death grip. My legs shook as we screamed through the cold winter night. After that I started riding regularly and got used to it. You couldn't and shouldn't do that today, but back then it was a different world. When I turned 18 I was eligible to become an auxiliary fireman, so I became legal.

In time I got my own gear including a helmet with a Ladder I64 frontispiece. My helmet came from my Dad who worked for the Consolidated Edison Electric Company. At some time in the past some Con Ed emergency crews had regulation fire helmets and he was able to get one for me.

I remember one run on Springfield Boulevard where I was standing around with the guys from Ladder 164, when two old Jewish ladies walked by. One lady looked us over and said, "Mine Got in Heaven Sadie, will you look at how young that fireman is." She was right, I was about 16 years old.

The Douglaston firehouse still does not see a lot of fire activity, but back then working fires were very unusual. In the 1950s I went on many runs and saw very few working structure fires. During that time I almost never saw fire from a structure, and very seldom saw smoke from one.

I remember two attic fires in those years, one in Little Neck and the other in Douglaston Manor. At the fire in the Manor upon arrival the Lieutenant shouted for me to assist John the MPO hook up to the hydrant. I did the wrong thing and dropped the hard sleeve from the pumper which actually slowed John down. I was embarrassed but I started learning a valuable lesson, how to keep yourself under control.

About half of all runs in those days were for brush fires, mostly in the swamp areas between Douglaston and Bayside. Occasionally some brush fires were extensive and could require up to six hours to control. I was not allowed inside structure fires, but I was a big help at brush fires with a broom or an indian pump, and that, along with my ice creams runs and my enthusiasm for the job and made me quite helpful.

In the early 1950s there was a fatal fire on Van Nostrand Court in Little Neck. Two children died in their beds during a daytime fire. I was not there but I remember seeing the medical examiner's hearse go by. It was big news at the time because fatal fires were so rare and there was controversy about a delayed response because of the unusual address. Several years ago there was another controversy for a delayed medical call on the same street.

There were no manning standards back then. Typically there would be three men on the back step and two on the side of the truck but it varied. Sometimes there would be one man on the back step and one driving the hose wagon. I remember one run when I was riding, when I was the only one on the side of the truck.

One night in 1955 I was in the sitting room of Engine 313, when a Bayside box, 6160 sounded on the bells. Very soon after, the distinctive 2-2 sounded, a second alarm for box 6160, 43rd Ave and Bell Blvd. There was a stunned silence. Lt Comiskey looked at the ringing bells and said "Oh my God." Probably the last 2nd alarm that they had was in 1948 when a small plane crashed into a house in Bayside. Going down Northern Blvd on the back step we could see a huge glow in the night sky. The fire was in a lumberyard across the Long Island Railroad tracks from E306. It would become a 5th alarm.

Later I asked John Gilday who had opened Engine 313 in 1929 whether 313 had ever been to a 5th before and he said never. In those days since neither company was assigned above a 2nd alarm and neither relocated, it is very unlikely that they were ever at a 3rd or 4th alarm before.

I sometimes spent the night at the firehouse. Most of the firemen were Catholic and I remember that some of them would say their prayers on their knees before getting into their bunk. Of the fifty firemen assigned to the Douglaston fire companies, all were married except for one who was divorced. It was a different era.

THE ARSONIST

It started in the fall of 1955. There was a small fire outside a garage about 5 blocks north of the firehouse. As time passed there was another small garage fire. Over the next year there were a few more, all were in the same neighborhood and all at night, but none were serious. Then one night the sky was lit up by a serious fire in a large vacant building that became a second alarm.

I had the advantage of working with all the shifts so it was easier for me to see a pattern. I noticed the same kid who I knew to be a problem always seemed to be at these fires. At the second alarm I told the lieutenant my suspicions and he questioned the suspect. His story of how he happened to be there didn't add up so the lieutenant spoke to the arson investigator who followed up. The kid wound up in some kind of reform school and the fires stopped. The story made the Long Island Star Journal newspaper.

THE DOUGLASTON FIRE COMPANIES APPEARING IN WNYF

The Douglaston companies have responded to some multiple alarms that have appeared in WNYF. The following articles have been abbreviated and are printed with permission.

THE BAYSIDE PLANE CRASH

The cover photo shown above shows firemen probing for victims in the ruins of a house where a Navy Corsair plane crashed on September 4, 1948. This fire occurred at Box 6192 located at 39th Avenue and 212th Street.The fireman in the center is Fireman Frances X. Baxter of Ladder 164, which responded as the second alarm truck. I heard the sirens from the Douglaston companies responding to this fire, and went down to Northern Boulevard expecting to see the Bayside companies. Instead I soon saw Engine 304's Ahrens Fox responding to Engine 313, which I realized was a relocation. I went to the firehouse and they confirmed that they were relocated on the second alarm, but since there were no radios, they had no idea about the fire.

Engine 304's Ahrens Fox Pumper
Photo by John Calderone, courtesy of WNYF

DOUGLASTON DISASTER

Article by Lawrence Fantoz, Deputy Chief, 14th, Division, FDNY

At 0124 hours on the morning of September 11,1979, Box 3935 Douglaston Parkway and 244th Street was transmitted for a fire in the Douglaston area of Queens.

For the firefighting forces of that area, it had been a quiet, uneventful evening. The weather had turned cool and the night was clear. It was also an evening that would not soon be forgotten; either by firefighting forces or residents of the area.

When members of the first arriving units approached Box 3935, there was little doubt in their minds that their firefighting expertise would be sorely tested battling this blaze. Waiting for them was a roaring inferno that was sweeping through eight new luxury homes that were under construction. The fire had already progressed to the point whereby radiant heat had set fire to six occupied homes located ninety-four feet to the north, and had ignited vehicles that were parked on the street. The radiant heat was so intense that the residents of those occupied exposures were unable to evacuate their homes through their front doors, and had to flee for their lives via rear exits.

CONDITIONS ON ARRIVAL

First arriving units encountered a tremendous volume of fire. The cockloft and top floors of the closest six exposed buildings (Exp. #I - see diagram) were already on fire. Flames were shooting through the roofs of the first four dwellings in that group. The structures to the east were smoking; their asphalt shingles on the mansard type roofs were melting.

117

The dwellings to the west (N.W. corner of 70th Avenue) were starting to burn at the roof level. The garage doors at some locations were burnt through. Grass, shrubbery, and railroad ties (used as retaining walls) were burning in front of the homes.

Twenty-eight motor vehicles that were parked on both sides of 70th Avenue, and in driveways, were involved in fire. Their gasoline tanks presented an explosion hazard but, fortunately, none of them ruptured. Burning tires on these vehicles were emitting an acrid, black smoke.

A large construction trailer, parked near the corner on the north side of 70th Avenue, at Douglaston Parkway, was completely engulfed in flames. Fire was billowing from its windows and burning through its walls. Overhead electric wires were arcing, accompanied by the ominous sound of exploding transformers. Many utility poles were on fire, with their power lines sagging dangerously. At the intersection of Douglaston Parkway and 70th Avenue, the power lines had sagged to a point where they were only eight feet above street level.

INITIAL OPERATIONS

First arriving units were met with a wall of searing heat, which prevented members or apparatus from entering the fire street. This condition required all responding units to position themselves on the perimeter of the fire area. They literally had to fight their way to the fire.

Lt. Ginal, commanding Engine Co. 313, the first unit to arrive, immediately transmitted a 2nd alarm. His company was unable to enter 70th Avenue due to the tremendous volume of fire. Lt. Ginal ordered his men to connect their pumper to a hydrant located on the west side of Douglaston Parkway, facing 70th Avenue. He then ordered the simultaneous stretching of a 2 1/2" hose-line and the operation of Engine 313's stang nozzle from atop their pumper. As his men advanced to the occupied structures (Exposure #1), the Stang nozzle provided them with a protective cooling cover of water. It was also able to knock down large bodies of fire on both sides of the street.

The members of Engine Co. 313 stretched their handline down 70th Ave amidst rubble and burned autos, past the burning construction trailer parked at the curb. They continued their advance on the burning occupied structures. As they advanced, they darkened the fire in their path. As the fire was darkened in one building, they advanced to the next. Working in close coordination with members of Engine Co. 313, the members of Engine 251, using one of their handlines, alternated their attack with that company, advancing building by building. Both companies continued working their way down to the end of the row of buildings that were on fire, and then through the alley to the rear.

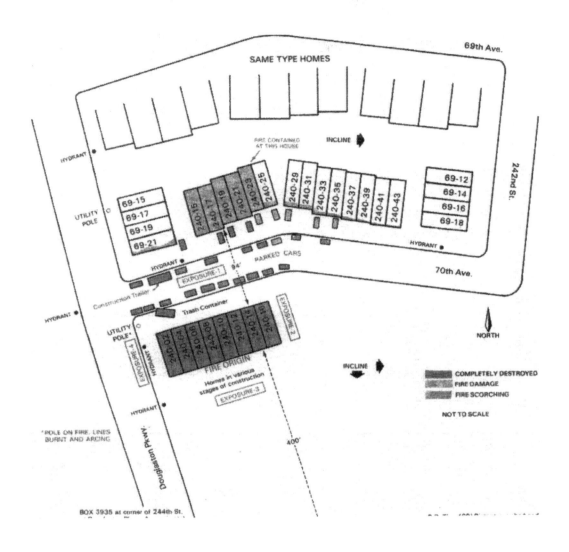

Diagram courtesy of WNYF

When Engine Co. 306 arrived, they followed up on Engine Co. 313's operations, alternating their stream; first on the involved buildings, then on the burning autos. The operation and advancement of all units on 70th Avenue continued.

All members operated under conditions of high radiant heat due to the heavy fire on both flanks, which was further intensified by all the cars burning in the street. Members of Ladder Company 164, the first due ladder company, entered the exposed buildings to perform primary search and ventilation, making certain that the occupants had reached safety. The exposed buildings were entered from the rear yard. They were searched and then vented in the rear. The front doors and windows were left intact to provide protection from the high heat being radiated from across the street.

3rd ALARM TRANSMITTED

When Battalion Chief Arthur J. Gordon, 53rd Batt. arrived at the scene, he immediately ordered the transmission of a 3rd alarm. Shortly after his arrival, and prior to the arrival of 3rd alarm units, the original fire buildings collapsed.

The most seriously exposed buildings comprising Exposure #1 were the six attached dwellings directly opposite the fire building, 94 feet away.

Hydrants in the area supplied copious amounts of water, under more than adequate pressures. Engine Company 313 reported an intake pressure of 80 PSI, allowing them to comfortably operate their Stang nozzle while they supplied two handlines.

As 3rd alarm units arrived, they were assigned the task of augmenting the heavy caliber appliances that were in operation. In addition, they stretched handlines to extinguish the fires that were still burning in many of the autos, and assisted firefighting forces inside occupied structures.

CONTROL

The construction of these buildings is not unlike the row frame dwellings with which Brooklyn is plagued. When final extinguishment and overhauling were completed in the occupied structures, two engine companies and one ladder company was assigned to overhaul the construction trailer and the cars in the street and alleyways. The fire was declared under control at 0300 hours; one hour and thirty-six minutes after the transmission of the initial alarm.

The aggressive attack by first arriving units; the prompt transmission of greater alarms; the more than adequate water supply; and the skillful deployment of fire resources were all key factors in limiting the spread of this fire.

Looking down 70th Avenue amidst burned autos and rubble
Photo courtesy of WNYF

Six-Alarm Brush Fire in Douglaston, Queens

by Deputy Chief Michael Giovinazzo

The 6 x 9 tour April 1st, 2000 was winding down at the 14th Division Headquarters. This was April Fools Day, a day for practical jokes. What was in the near future with the transmission of Box 8384 was no joke.

Upon the transmission of the l0-75 signal by Engine 313, reporting a brush fire at the Long Island Expressway (LIE) and the northbound Cross Island Parkway (CIP), Division 14 responded immediately.

From the LIE, at Flushing Meadow Park, Deputy Chief Michael Giovinazzo observed a mushroom of black smoke filling the sky. He and his aide were still more than six miles away. While responding, the Deputy Chief's intuition told him that what was unfolding had more potential than just a brush fire.

ARRIVAL AT THE BOX LOCATION

As Division 14 approached the area where operations were being set up along the ramp from the LIE to the northbound CIP, Chief Giovinazzo noted that the first three engine companies were in the process of relaying water to attack the fire. His field of vision was little more than a thick line of trees in front of him and a sky full of black smoke. As he attempted to gain information to implement a strategy, the Chief was greeted by FF Terrence McMahon, the Chauffeur of Engine 313. FF McMahon calmly and concisely provided a picture of what was burning, where the fire was going and what the structural exposures were. Specifically, Chief Giovinazzo was provided with the following information, verbally and by viewing a map.

The fire area was part of Alley Pond Park, an area about 1/2 mile wide by 3/4 of a mile deep. The area is bounded by Northern Boulevard on the north, the CIP on the west, the LIE on the south and Hanford Street, which continues to 240th Street, on the east.

The main life and property hazards were the private dwellings on Hanford Street and 240th Street which ran on a ridge above the fire and the commercial occupancies on the south side of Northern Boulevard, from 231 Street to Alameda Avenue.

Most of the fire area could not be reached by hose-lines. Chief Giovinazzo now had the information necessary to implement a strategy to protect life and structural property.

STRATEGY

All second-alarm units under the command of Battalion 52 were directed to respond to Hanford Street - the exposure #2 side-the most critical side of the fire. This sector later was filled out with additional units and further sectored, as were all the other sectors eventually. It was imperative to gain an immediate foothold in all sectors and then reinforce them.

The exposure #3 side, continuing onto half of the exposure #4 side, was under the command of Battalion 20. This sector contained no structures, but needed protection because of exposure to the northbound CIP, which subsequently was closed to traffic. This sector was staffed by first- and some third-alarm units.

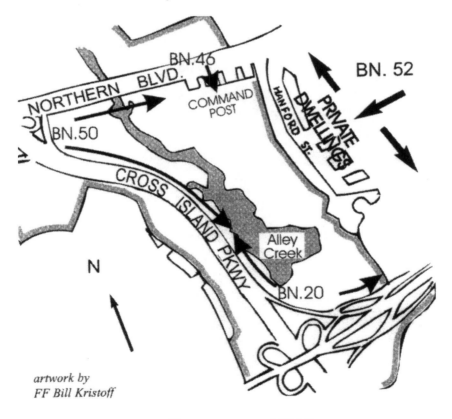

Diagram courtesy of WNYF

The exposure #4 side was from the Battalion 20 sector to the western part of exposure #1, commanded by Battalion 50. This sector contained a one-story structure used by the Department of Environmental Protection. This structure soon became exposed and protecting it became a priority.

The remainder of exposure #1, where it met exposure #2, was commanded by Battalion 46. This was also a critical sector because of the commercial occupancies on Northern Boulevard.

A NYPD helicopter was requested immediately upon realization of the inaccessibility of much of the fire area. The final part of the strategy was to employ the helicopter with the water basket to attack areas inaccessible to operating units. The helicopter was refilled from nearby Little Neck Bay. This helicopter was manned by an FDNY Battalion Chief. This Chief was in constant handie-talkie communications with the Command Post.

*all photos this page
by FF J.J. Brown*

The NYPD Helicopter with it's water basket
Photo courtesy of WNYF

TACTICS

The tactics employed by units were many and varied:
Long hose stretches
Satellite monitor
Tower ladder streams
Indian pumps
Rattan brooms
Reconnaissance patrols
Observation from tower ladders and high ground

Firefighters operating at the Douglaston brush fire
WNYF photo by F/F J. J. Brown

DAMAGE

Remarkably, the only damage caused as a result of this fire was to cars parked at the vegetation line, behind the automobile dealership, on Northern Boulevard.

ACKNOWLEDGEMENTS

Special recognition is extended to FF Terrence McMahon of Engine 313. His initiative and relay of critical information at the right time prevented a disaster. Battalion Chief Jack Corcoran, the Commander of Battalion 52, excelled in commanding the critical side of this fire. Assistant Chief Frank Cruthers, the City-Wide Tour Commander, assumed operational command.

Last, but certainly not least, are the fire companies who implemented the grand plan. At this fire, the potential for disaster was great. The limited damage sustained at this fast-moving fire is testimony to the initiatives taken and the capabilities and effort expended by the fire companies. Once again, the operating units upheld FDNY's proud tradition of selfless service for the protection of life and property.

Chronology of Alarm--Overview		
Signal	*Ordered By*	*Time*
8384	CADS	1540
10-84	E-313	1545
10-75	E-313	1550
10-84	Bn-52	1602
10-84	Bn-20	1606
10-84	Div. 14	1606
2-2	Div. 14	1610
3-3	Div. 14	1620
4-4	Div. 14	1642
5-5	Div. 14	1644
6 additional Engines	Car 4C	1713
Probably Will Hold	Car 4C	1845
Under Control	Car 4C	1928

SEPTEMBER 11th, 2001

On the morning of September 11th, 2001, hijackers flew two jet planes into the World Trade Center (WTC), one into each tower in a coordinated terrorist attack. After burning for 56 minutes, the South Tower collapsed, followed a half-hour later by the North Tower. Large planes with long flights were selected for hijacking because they would be heavily fueled. The attacks resulted in the deaths of 2,606 people in the towers and on the ground. The FDNY lost 343 firefighters. There were 75 firehouses in which at least one member was killed.

The response of the FDNY to the World Trade Center was unprecedented in scale and scope. In the first three hours alone, six-fifth alarms and a second alarm were transmitted. Their efforts were supplemented by numerous off-duty firefighters and emergency medical technicians.

Retired FDNY Firefighter Bob Beckwith saw the South Tower collapse on television. Even though he had been had been retired from Tower Ladder I64 for seven years, he grabbed his old gear and went past the blockades and barricades that had been set up and began helping with searches.

When President Bush arrived, a secret service agent asked Beckwith to help the President onto a rubble pile. Beckwith handed President Bush a bullhorn to address the crowd of responders and workers and was told to climb down by the Secret Service, but President Bush insisted that Beckwith stay with him.

President Bush and Firefighter Bob Beckwith TL 164 (Retired)

President George W. Bush in response to the crowds chants of USA, USA, USA said: "I can hear you. The rest of the world hears you and the people who knocked these buildings down will hear from all of us soon."

In my wildest dreams I never thought that I would see the President of the United States with his arm around a Ladder 164 firefighter, standing on the rubble where 343 FDNY firefighters died. I still can't believe it.

Engine 313 and Tower Ladder 164 did not respond to the initial alarms, they relocated to fill vacant firehouses. During the following months, they along with all the other fire companies in the city spent many tours working at the World Trade Center.

The FDNY operated around-the-clock at the WTC site until the end of May 2002. Many firefighters were exposed to WTC related dust and fumes which caused respiratory, sinus, asthma and lung problems. The FDNY has found that nearly 9,000 firefighters with WTC exposure may be at greater risk for cancer than firefighters who weren't exposed.

A Memorial Wall has been established at FDNY Headquarters that is dedicated to those who died after 9/11 as a result of exposure to toxic materials. This Wall shows that the sacrifices that FDNY members made on September 11, 2001, did not end on that day. The then Chief of Department Edward Kilduff stated "The work they did was noble and selfless. We gave our all on 9/11 and we continue to give to this day."

The memorial wall honoring the fallen firefighters
Photo courtesy of WNYF

The inscription on the Memorial Wall reads:

DEDICATED TO THE MEMORY OF THOSE WHO BRAVELY SERVED THIS DEPARTMENT PROTECTING LIFE AND PROPERTY IN THE CITY OF NEW YORK IN THE RESCUE AND RECOVERY EFFORT AT MANHATTAN BOX 5-5-8087 WORLD TRADE CENTER.

THE LITTLE NECK COMMERCIAL FIRE

The all hands commercial fire pictured below occurred in a store at 253-35 Northern Boulevard on September 8, 2007. Engine 313 and Tower Ladder 164 were first due.

Photo courtesy of WNYF

Queens Gas Explosion
by Battalion Chief Lawrence Blieka

April 24, 2009 was a beautiful spring day, with sunny skies. The Queens dispatcher transmitted Box 6773 at 1650 hours for a report of a building explosion. The first alarm assignment was Engines 251, 313, 326 TL 164, TL162 and Battalion 53.

As Chief Blieka, Battalion 53 turned down Union Turnpike still some two miles from the reported explosion a very large column of smoke could be seen in the distance. At this point, Lieutenant Timothy Keenan, Engine 251, transmitted a 10-75, based on the smoke condition and the fact that he and his members had felt the impact of the explosion in quarters approximately eight blocks away.

Immediately on arrival at the Box, Engine 251 transmitted a I0-60 (major emergency response), followed by a second alarm, at 1654 and 1655 hours, respectively.

Chief Blieka arrived at 1657 hours and was met with the following conditions:

A very heavy odor of natural gas permeated the outside atmosphere on 260th Street from 79th to 80th Avenues.

A two-story private dwelling at 80-50 260th Street, was fully involved in fire, with the first and second floors pancaked onto its foundation, due to a natural gas explosion.

Exposure #2, also a two-story private dwelling, had sustained significant structural damage to its #4 side and had heavy fire in the basement and first and second floors.

Exposure #4, a similar private dwelling, had sustained significant structural damage to its #2 side and had heavy fire on the first and second floors.

Exposure #3 had sustained structural damage to its rear and its detached garage from the explosion.

On arrival, Chief Bliek deployed the rest of the first-alarm assignment as illustrated.

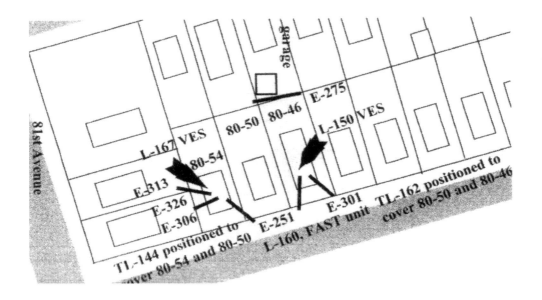

Diagram courtesy of WNYF

INITIAL OPERATIONS

Engine 251 members were aggressively protecting exposures, and resultant radiant heat. While operating on the Exposure #2 building, one of Engine 251's off-duty members, FF Anthony Conte, observed a disoriented elderly woman in one of the windows. Under the protection of a 2 1/2 inch hose line, he entered the occupancy and removed the 87-year-old female, just before the building becoming completely engulfed in fire.

Engine 313 stretched and operated a 2 1/2 inch hose line into the second floor of Exposure #2, Ladder 164 performed VES (Vent, Enter, Search) of Exposure #4.

Second-alarm ladder companies along with Haz-Mat with their meters completed the searches and evacuated all houses on 260th Street between 80th and 81st Avenues.

With doubts about the structural stability of both Exposures #2 and #4 and because of damage from the explosion and the heavy fire load, all interior operations halted and a tower ladder operation was set up. Final extinguishment was completed with two tower ladder streams and handlines operating from the exterior. The fire was declared under control at 2116 hours.

CONCLUSION:

Early and appropriate transmission of alarms (l0-60, second alarm) at this expanding operation was vital in providing the required manpower and technical resources to successfully extinguish this fire.

THE THROGS NECK BRIDGE FIRE
WNYF article by Deputy Assistant Chief Robert Maynes

In the early morning hours of Friday, July 10, 2009, vacationers and commuters attempting to leave Long Island were presented with an astounding image. Visible from the westbound Cross Island Parkway, just past Fort Totten, was 50 feet of flames, originating approximately 10 feet below the roadway of the Throgs Neck Bridge (TNB). By the end of the day, more than 300 first responders from multiple agencies operated to prevent the loss of the bridge.

On July 10th, overnight crews were working below the Bronx bound span. In order to prevent any loose debris (concrete, asphalt, etc.) from falling into the water, the bridge contractors constructed a wood deck by laying wood lengths side by side between the webs of the I-beams. This is called a debris deck. Additionally, protective netting spanned approximately 500 feet of the scaffolding. The netting and deck provided for personal and environmental safety but also introduced a serious fire load to a steel structure.

As a precaution, a standpipe was included in the TNB construction to be fed by engine companies assigned to the Bronx end of the bridge. A standpipe outlet for fire suppression was located at the top of the main span.

When the fire started construction workers were using a liquefied petroleum gas. The incipient fire accidentally started in the scaffolding area approximately 350 feet from the Queens entrance to the Bronx bound TNB. Initially, construction workers attempted to extinguish the fire using hand extinguishers.

The delayed alarm attempts hindered FDNY operations and fed by a 10 mph northeast wind, the fire rapidly intensified and extended to all exposed materials, including the netting and platform. As the fire progressed, two 100-pound cylinders of MAPP gas were exposed. A subsequent BLEVE (boiling liquid expanding vapor explosion) occurred. The BLEVE intensified the fire and created two approximately six- by six-foot diameter holes in the decking.

The uncontrolled fire was severely impacting stability of the bridge, and with commuters crossing the bridge, collapse or permanent loss of the bridge was a distinct possibility.

First-alarm units were confronted with a complex operation that required discipline and outside-the-box decisions. Engine 295 arrived first, responding north bound from Queens. A signal 10-75 was promptly transmitted at 0530 hours.

Chief Crichton, Battalion 52's size-up included an advanced fire in an undetermined area below the bridge roadway. The fire was increasing and moving northerly toward the midspan. The extent of damage to the structural steel of the bridge was unknown. Initial reports were that there was no life hazard, which meant that the suppression resources being introduced were the life hazard. FDNY Marine resources were responding, but did not arrive for 30 minutes. The stability of the access below the roadway to the fire area was questionable.

Engine 295 started knocking down fire in the open area between the deck platform and the underside of the bridge roadway. Water supply to handlines required below the bridge also proved to be a complex operation. Battalion Chief John Maguire, Battalion 54, was assigned as Water Supply Group Supervisor, and 10 companies were assigned the task of laying 16 lengths of 3 1/2- inch supply line. Simultaneously, Engine 295 was being fed by engines serving as water tenders that were emptying their booster tanks into Engine 295's booster tank and returning to a hydrant to replenish their supply. Continuous water was successfully supplied to Engine 295 waiting for the 3 1/2 - inch supply line, which was being stretched. Chief Crichton transmitted a second alarm at 0540 hours. Engine 313 responded on the second alarm.

Firefighters attacking the Throgs Neck Bridge Fire
Photo courtesy of WNYF

Marine 6 now was on-scene in the East River below the fire area. It used its stream from the East River directed at the platform and the debris deck. The result was a significant reduction in fire volume and heat. Due to the combination of the handline stream, followed by the large-caliber Marine 6 stream, the majority of the fire was knocked down and the temperature of the steel was returned to normal.

Marine 6's stream from it's 2500 GPM monitor
Photo by FF David Raynor, SOC
Photo courtesy of WNYF

Rescue 3, with support from Squads 288 and 270, constructed a rope safety line and all suppression forces hooked themselves into the rope and performed operations from the safety line. Extinguishment of the fire required a handline operated by tethered Squad personnel.

Final extinguishment was concluded at 1459 hours. The Special Operations Group used the services of two Rescue and four Squad companies, in addition to the third-alarm assignment, called at 0606 hours.

The extent of damage was investigated by engineers. At 1400 hours, a determination was made by all cooperating agencies to open the Queens-bound span. The Bronx-bound span required 30 days of repair before full use was restored.

CONCLUSION

FDNY resources were faced with a complex incident requiring critical decisions. The units operated in a professional manner based on appropriate incident priorities. Serious injuries were prevented, while completing complex operations and preventing catastrophic loss of an important suspension bridge.

Queens
Transformer Fire
Prompts Use of
New Technologies

by Deputy Chief Kubler

THE DOUGLASTON TRANSFORMER FIRE

On July 24th, 2009, Deputy Chief Kubler, Division 14, heard Box 6334 transmitted for a car accident at the intersection of 244th Street and Northern Boulevard. What seemed like a moment later, he heard the officer of Engine 313 tell the dispatcher that they did not have a car accident but, instead, a transformer fire.

The engine officer, Lieutenant John Downey, in command of Engine 313 transmitted a 10-75 signal, quickly sized up the situation and realized the potential for fire spread from the transformer to Exposure #4, a three-story commercial building. With this in mind he ordered the placement of Engine 313's apparatus to the south side of Northern Boulevard and the deck gun of the apparatus was placed into operation while a handline simultaneously was stretched to provide exposure protection.

On arrival, the second, third and fourth due engine companies stretched and operated handlines to protect the exposures buildings. While en route to the Box location and still some distance away, Deputy Chief Kubler heard Battalion 53 give a preliminary report that they were operating using four lines. Hearing this transmission, Chief Kubler ordered a second alarm for the Box at 0805 hours. Although not on the scene, the reason for this action was obvious. If four lines are in operation with just an All Hands assignment, there would be no reserve units to do anything else.

All units that were operating lines were careful not to place water on the involved transformer. While engine companies were protecting exposures with hose-lines, ladder companies were busy searching all exposures for possible extension of fire, as well as evacuating occupancies where there was a possibility of exposure to smoke from the transformer.

As additional units arrived, the operation was sectored and Haz-Mat 1 and Squad 288 performed atmospheric readings throughout the operation to check on LEL (lower explosive limit) levels.

While waiting for confirmation of power off and as units arrived, a number of lines were stretched for foam operations. The Satellite unit set up the manifold and Ladder 152 and Tower Ladder 164 were supplied.

Operations at the Douglaston transformer fire
Photo courtesy of WNYF

A third alarm was transmitted at 0854 hours for logistical reasons. The Chiefs knew the operation would last a while (the incident was placed under control at 1049 hours) and they wanted to be able to replace units as needed. After gathering intelligence on-scene, the course of action to follow was determined. First, the Purple K would be used to knock down the fire. Once this had been accomplished, a new technology, F-500, would be used by Haz-Mat 1 via a handline. The purpose of F-500 is to remove heat. If additional resources were needed, the foam lines would be put into operation.

Finally, conventional foam was applied to try to prevent the areas that the Purple K had extinguished from re-igniting. This proved successful, with a foam blanket applied.

As a necessary precaution, all FDNY members exposed to the water were decontaminated prior to leaving and had their bunker gear taken for decon.

Good initial tactics by first-arriving units can make all the difference. At this operation, Engine 313 the first-due engine knew that protecting exposures was a priority and Engine 313's officer issued the proper orders to make sure that it was done.

AN UNBELIEVABLE DAY

July 7, 2010, started off as a typical summer day with New York City in the grips of a heat wave and the day's forecast offered no relief with temperatures expected to reach 90+ degrees. The FDNY unfortunately, was in the middle of what would turn out to be one of its busiest fire duty days in many years.

There were only five fifth alarms in all of New York City in 2012 which is about average. The odds of two fifth alarms on the same day are long. The odds are much longer that they would be on the same day in the same borough.

On July 7th, 2010, there were two fifth alarms in Queens. The first began at 1021 hours in the Woodhaven section. At 1126 hours a fifth alarm was transmitted and Tower Ladder l64 responded from relocation to the 5th alarm.

THE RUN SHEET:
Woodhaven 5th alarm

5-5 4613 @ 11:26
Eng. 301 act. 319. 271, 260, 16 act. 289
Lad. 42 act.136, T. Lad 164 acting T Lad. 138

A few hours later at 1441 hours the same day, box 3761 was transmitted for a fire in the Bayside section of Queens and Engine 313 was a first alarm engine. By 1540 a 5th alarm had been transmitted. In the 1950s it was inconceivable that E313 & L164 would ever be operating at two separate 5th alarms at the same time. Actually it's unbelievable today.

This reminds me that during my 31 year career with the Washington D.C. Fire Department there was one major plane crash and one major Metro subway crash. They both happened three hours apart on January 13th, 1982.

Units throughout Division 14 still were recovering from an earlier fifth alarm fire when an alarm was received, reporting a fire at l8-15 215th Street. Dispatchers sent a full assignment of three engines, two trucks and a Battalion to respond to the Box.

It was an unusual beginning for the Bayside five alarmer, few 5th alarms start with the first-arriving units seeing nothing and asking for a verification of the address. The dispatcher relayed to units new information, that the caller saw smoke coming from the roof of a building on Bell Boulevard.

FDNY Battles Summer Heat and Queens Five-Alarm Fire

by Deputy Chief Mark Cuccurullo

Ladder 167 arrived first at the building at 16-66 Bell Boulevard a 16 story, Class 1, multiple dwelling and saw what appeared to be smoke emanating from the roof. Being proactive because of summer heat and prior experience with this building, Engine 320 transmitted a 10-70 (water supply is required) recognizing the building's isolated location and a lack of a positive water supply on this street. Engine 320's initiative to transmit the 10-70 via an urgent message and Engine 313 assuming the water resource unit responsibilities played important roles, leading to the successful operation at this fire. It prevented any delay in getting water.

When Ladder 167 arrived at the roof level they noticed smoke pushing from the roof ventilation fans. Suddenly, the roof gave way, causing FF Kevin Larkin, of Ladder 167 to fall waist-deep into the cockloft. Ladder 167's lieutenant proceeded to try to assist the firefighter. Then, he too fell knee-deep into the cockloft. Recognizing that he was near a fire division wall, he was able to self-extricate himself and help the firefighter out of the hole. The officer then notified the battalion that there was a heavy fire condition in the cockloft.

Chief Duffy, Battalion 52 immediately transmitted a second alarm at 1458 hours. Reports from the roof indicated a heavy fire condition through the roof existing above three apartments on the exposure #2 side of the building.

Units continued to battle the fire, when a mayday transmission was broadcast by the chauffeur of Ladder 167, indicating he was trapped on the roof, near the front of the building on the exposure #2 side, and the FAST truck staged on the sixth floor was deployed.

Within minutes, Ladder 160, assisted by Rescue 4 members, arrived at the location of the trapped member and reported back that the chauffeur was in-hand, being placed on a backboard. He was removed to EMS personnel.

With resources allocated for the removal of the trapped member and fire conditions worsening, Chief Sudnik transmitted a third alarm at 1503 hours and established a Command Channel. Fire units continued working to get a handle on fire conditions. Searches of the fire building were paramount. Due to the numerous occupants and with resources at a premium, many of them elderly with physical limitations who were in no danger were sheltered in place in their apartments, rather than expose them to the crowded and debris filled hallways and stairwells. These elderly occupants were checked periodically to ensure their safety.

With conditions continuing to worsen on the top floor and roof and fresh units in short supply, Chief Sudnik transmitted a fourth alarm at 1511 hours, anticipating the future need for resources. He kept in mind that this was the second multiple alarm in Queens that day and that the reflex time (the elapsed time from recognition of the need for additional units to the time the requested units arrive on-scene) and are in position to operate would be impacted, due to their response from long distances. Companies continued to aggressively battle fire conditions with engines operating six handlines off two standpipe risers

Four lines were operating on the fire floor and two lines were operating on the roof, while truck companies used hooks and saws to expose the fire. Fire conditions began to darken down and the advantage began to swing in the FDNY's favor. Primary searches were complete and negative and secondary searches were underway.

At 1540 hours, Chief Sweeney transmitted a fifth alarm to relieve operating units and bring in fresh units in preparation for the overhaul phase of the fire. Chief Sweeney declared the incident probably will hold at 1626 hours and after all secondary searches were completed, he placed the fire under control at 1643 hours. In spite of brutal weather conditions a 90+ degree day with high humidity and the fact that fire conditions were well advanced prior to FDNY arrival, units operated as hard as they could for as long as possible. The constant awareness of members physical condition, as well as the resources available, were of great importance. Rotating and relieving members was a priority for the I.C.

Firefighters operating at the Bayside 5th alarm
Photo courtesy of WNYF

Companies operating at this fire were subjected to severe conditions, both inside the occupancy and outside. Engine 313 got beat up as they alone had several rooms of fire going in one of multiple apartments on the top floor. Due to the companies professionalism, dedication and sheer determination, damage to the building, as well as civilian injuries, were kept to a minimum.

THE RUN SHEET FOR THE BAYSIDE FIFTH ALARM:

Bayside Queens, N. Y. 07/07/10

Box 3731 14:41 16-66 Bell Blvd. & 18th Ave.

Engs. 320, 313, 274, Lad.167, T. Lad. 144 Batt. 52

10- 75- 3731 @ 14:57

TowerLadder 160 is designated as the "FAST" Truck, Eng. 326, Rescue 4, Squad 288, Batt. 53, Division 14

2nd Alarm @ 14:58

Engs. 299, 297, 205 act. 289, 298, Lad.129, Lad. 125, Eng. 291 w/ Satellite 4, Batt. 50 "Safety Officer" Batt. 39 act. 46 "Resource Unit Leader"

3rd alarm @ 15:03

Eng. 89, 295 act. 305, 331 act. 273, 314 act. 315 Lad. 151, Lad. 150. Batt. 54. Batt. 51 "Staging Manager" Batt. 43 "Air Re-Con Chief," Staging Area: Bell Blvd. 23rd Ave.

Special Call

Eng. 312 act. 307, Eng. 304 w/ High Rise Nozzle, Eng. 39 w/ High Rise 1, Safety Battalion

4th Alarm @ 15:11

Engs. 275, 251, 317, 308 T. Lad. 155 act. 162, T. Lad.138, Batt. 38 act. 52, Batt. 17 act. 52 "Planning Chief," Batt. 20, & Car 4: Chief Robert Sweeney, "Chief of Operations." Eng. 262 with Planning Vehicle

5th Alarm@15:40

Engs. 225 act. 316, 314 act. 299, 332 act. 273, 258 act. 274 Lad. 123 act. 150, T. Lad. 54 act. T. Lad. 160. Tower Ladder 152 s/c as another "FAST" Truck

15:46 Special Call an additional Rescue & an additional Squad, Rescue 3 & Squad 61 are assigned.

15:48 Special Call (2) more additional Truck Co's.
Tower Ladder 127 & Ladder 133 are s/c

15:55 Progress Report for the 5th alarm Box 3731, Car 4, Chief Sweeney reports: (6) hand - lines stretched and in operation. Fire involves 4 apartments on the top floor with extension into the cockloft above the apartments involved. Truck Co's are continuing to "Open Up." Fire remains doubtful.

16:05 Special Call (4) additional Trucks.
T. Lad. 162. Lad. 148 act. 126, Lad. 134 act. 143, Lad. 16 act. 151

16:26 Progress Report for the 5th alarm, Box 3731, Car 4, Chief Sweeney reports:
Main body of the fire has been knocked down.

1631 Special Call (2) additional Battalion Chief's
Batt. 32 act. 52, Batt act.?

16:43 Progress Report for the 5th alarm, Box 3731, Car 4, Chief Sweeney reports: Main body of fire has been extinguished. Special Call (3) Engine's & (3) Trucks for "relief"

Engs. 268, 237, 279 act. 277, Lad. 110 act. 107, Lad. 106, Lad. 173

(Job Duration: 2 hrs/ 1 min)

A total of 24 engines, 21 ladders and 11 battalion chiefs operated at this fire.

Note that the two major fires resulted in many units from other boroughs responding to the Bayside 5th alarm fire. These companies were:

Manhattan:

Engine 39 and Tower Ladder 16 Lenox Hill - East side

Bronx:

Engine 89 Schuylerville, Tower Ladder 54 Clason Point, Battalion 17 Morrisania, Battalion 20 Westchester, Rescue 3 Tremont and Squad 61 Westchester

Brooklyn;

Engine 205 Brooklyn Heights, Engine 225 New Lots, Engine 279 Red Hook, Engine 332 East New York, Ladder 106 Greenpoint, Ladder 110 Downtown Brooklyn, Ladder 123 Crown Heights, Ladder 148 Borough Park, Battalion 32 Red Hook, Battalion 38 Crown Heights, Battalion 39 New Lots and Battalion 43 Coney island

HURRICANE SANDY

Hurricane Sandy occurred on October 29, 2012 and this storm became one the largest ever Atlantic hurricanes in size and flooding. Engine 313 and Tower Ladder 164 as most Queens companies were heavily involved in handling the floods, downed wires, wind damage and other problems caused by the hurricane.

The Rockaway section of Queens bore the brunt of the hurricanes wrath resulting in a conflagration that tore through 111 buildings, resulting in massive rescue operations. In addition thousands of homes and businesses were flooded.

Most of the Rockaway fire hydrants were underwater. This resulted in extensive water relays involving companies from all over the city. One relay consisted of Engine 96 from the Clason Point area of the Bronx, drafting water and supplying

Engine 247 from the Borough Park section of Brooklyn, who supplied Engine 14 from the Union Square section of Manhattan, that supplied water to Engine 329 the first due engine at the Breezy Point fire.

In the aftermath, the Douglaston companies along with many others were rotated periodically into the Rockaways to assist in handling the massive damage that the area suffered.

DOUGLASTON 3rd ALARM HOUSE FIRE

On the evening of August 14th, 2012, a major fire occurred in the very upscale Douglaston Manor section. It was apparently started by workmen in one of the houses. Engine 313 and Tower Ladder 164 arrived first due to find a rapidly spreading wall of flame. One very large building was heavily involved in fire and had already spread to exposure 4. A 10-75 and a second alarm were quickly transmitted.

The Douglaston 3rd alarm house fire at 3912 Douglaston Parkway
Photo by FF Michael Gomez, Squad 288 WNYF

After the arrival of Battalion 53 the fire spread to exposure 2, and a third alarm was transmitted. The fire was on the only road that leads directly into the Manor, causing a limited access that hampered the fire attack. The only way to come into the fire from the opposite side was by way of a little known back road, a several mile detour. Tower ladders and numerous handlines were used to finally bring this fire under control.

THE RUN SHEET

Queens, N.Y. Douglaston Section

Box 6340 Douglaston Parkway and 40th Avenue.

19:51
Engs 313, 326, 299, TL 164, TL 160, Batt. 53

19:53
10-75
Eng. 299, TL 152, SQ 288, Batt 52, Div 14

19:55
Second Alarm

Engs 320, 274, 301, 306, L150, L 167 E324, Rescue 4, Batt 50, Batt 54, TSU 1

20:04
Batt. 53 reports: 2 story vacant building, 20 x 100 fully involved. Fire heavily involves Exposure 4, a private dwelling. We have 3 lines in operation. Fire is doubtful will hold.

20:06
Bat. 53 reports: Transmit a third alarm, we have fire extension into another exposure.

Third Alarm

Engs. 273, 315, 298, 295, L 129, TL 162 Batt 51, Batt 49, Batt 33, MSU 1, Fieldcom, Car 4

20:32

Division 14 reports, 2 tower ladders and 4 handlines operating. Fire is darkening down. Still doubtful.

20:54 Fieldcom 1 reports: Fire under control.

DOUGLASTON 2nd ALARM HOUSE FIRE

At 16:30 hours on September 29th, 2014, Engine 313 and Tower Ladder 164 were dispatched first due to Box 6359 for a structure fire at 129 Ridge Road.

Upon arrival heavy smoke was showing from the upper stories of a large three story house and a 10-75 was transmitted. As the fire progressed a second alarm was transmitted and the strategy changed to an exterior operation using Tower Ladders 164 and 160 to knock down the fire. Six firefighters were injured fighting this fire and it took 1 hour and 37 minutes to place this fire under control.

Queens second alarm fire Box 2-2 6359 129 Ridge Road
Photo courtesy of Mike Gannon

CHAPTER 15

ENGINE 313 AND TOWER LADDER 164 TODAY

The Douglaston companies have been in service for 86 years. There has been a constant turnover of personnel and and I estimate that about 1500 firemen, 200 lieutenants and 50 captains have been assigned to the firehouse through the years. The average ages of the firemen today is about 40 years, a little less than years ago, probably because of the massive losses and retirements following 9/11.

Through the years they have had about 50,000 runs. The runs never stop, here is Engine 313 turning out on a response.

The gear has gotten much better and much heavier. The increased bulk of the gear has caused the gear rooms to expand out onto the apparatus floor as shown.

Meals and camaraderie are important. Here the guys are shown below preparing a meal.

The TV is still in the same place as the original black and white, but is now a large color flat screen.

The officers still grind out reports from the company office pictured below except now it is by computer, not a typewriter which has made it much easier. I can still hear the sounds of the typewriter, click, click, long pause click, then "Dammit" and the sound of paper yanked from the machine and crumpled.

The watch room has changed and the bells are gone, replaced by computer dispatch and response tones.

The watch room dispatch board

The company numbers displayed over the watch room
Photo by Jimmy Raftery FDNY Dispatcher

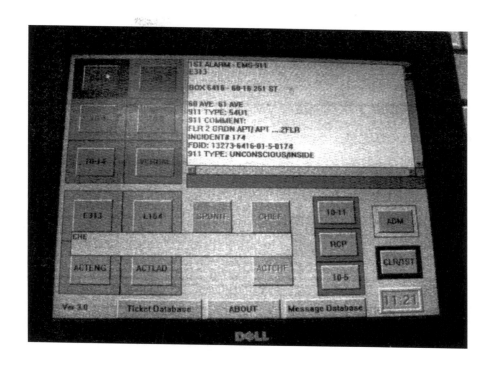

Alarms are dispatched by computer

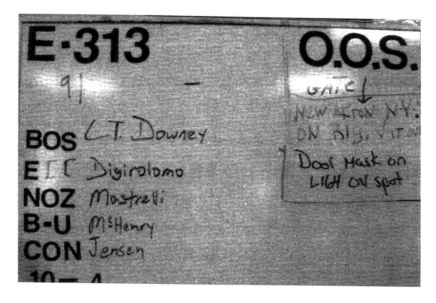

Engine 313's status board

The positions and assignments on the apparatus are formalized on the company status board, and a riding list shows who is on the apparatus and the jobs that they are assigned. The duties of the various positions are:

The officer: Keep tracks of his company and leads them at fires

The engine chauffeur: In charge of driving the pumper and operating the pump

The nozzle position: Advances the hose into the burning building

The backup firefighter: Helps the nozzle firefighter

The door/control position: Helps hook up the hoses and keeps the hose free of kinks and insures that the correct amount of hose is stretched.

Below is the company patch for Engine 313 and Ladder 164

FIREFIGHTING TODAY

How does firefighting in Douglaston today compare to the 1950s. The short answer is that today's firefighting is much better. Water is quicker, the pumpers carry water and pre-connected 1 3/4 inch hose, the ladders have gone from wood to metal, the aerials are hydraulic and there are many tower ladders. Turnout gear is much better, firefighters have SCBA, portable radios, manning is more consistent, and everybody rides inside the apparatus.

There are computers in the apparatus. A critical Information system (CIDS) provides vital information about specific buildings to help fire operations and improve safety. Fires are attacked using standard operating procedures and the incident command system uses sectors to improve the control and management of incidents. Units and functions are tracked on a command board and safety officers are assigned at serious fires.

Structure responses today are heavier as shown:

<u>1956</u>
E313 E306 L164 L152 BC53

<u>Today</u>
E313 E326 E306 TL164 L160 BC53

In addition when there are multiple phone calls, a 4th engine, a rescue and a squad are normally dispatched.

Additional responses for a 10-75, a working fire

<u>1956</u>
D.C.14

<u>Today</u>
E251, L167 (FAST Truck), BC 52, Rescue 4, Squad 288, D.C. 14

Multiple alarm responses include 4 engines, 2 trucks, a satellite engine company (for water supply), additional battalion chiefs for firefighting, safety, resource management, staging and air reconnaissance and for other specialized functions as needed. Special units responding include Tactical Support units (carrying specialized tools), and a RAC (recuperation, rehabilitation and care) unit.

SPECIALIZED TRAINING

The members of Engine 313 are trained as emergency medical technicians and the engine is a first responder to medical emergencies.

Tower Ladder 164 is trained as a cold water rescue unit. They are equipped with cold water rescue suits and other related equipment for responses to cold water and ice rescue incidents along the shoreline.

Tower Ladder 164 is also trained and equipped as a FAST truck (Firefighter Assist and Search Team). The FAST truck at a fire stands by in case a firefighter becomes trapped, lost or injured, and they are tasked with locating and removing them to safety.

FIRE COMPANY LOCATION CHANGES

Through the years in the Douglaston area some companies have been added, moved or been disbanded as the following maps show

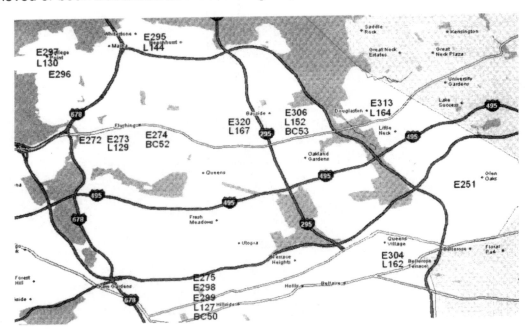

1955 firehouse locations in northeast Queens
Map courtesy of Ignatius Kapalczynskl

Engine 251 was established in1952

In 1960, Engine 299 and Ladder 152 moved into a new firehouse in the Fresh Meadows area. Engine 299 moved from the big house in Jamaica (explanation of the big house is found later in the Lingo Section) and Ladder 152 was moved from the quarters of Engine 306.

Engine 296 in College Point was disbanded in 1961 and Engine 272 in Flushing was disbanded in 1974

Engine 326 & Ladder 160 were established in 1984 and Battalion 53 moved there from the quarters of Engine 306 the same year. Since 1960 Queens has lost 4 engines and gained 3 engines and 3 truck companies.

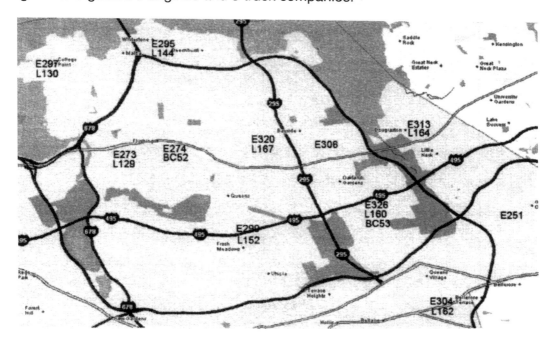

2015 firehouse locations in northeast Queens
Map courtesy of Ignatius Kapalczynskl

RESPONSES TODAY

As mentioned previously, neither Engine 313 or Ladder 164 ever relocated and they were not assigned above a second alarm. This all changed when Engine 326 and Ladder 160 were established and computers changed the dispatch system. Now the Douglaston companies can and do go all over the city on fires or relocations. Some examples:

2/2/93 0410 hours at a 5th alarm, 5-5 848 at Park Avenue and 48th Street, Manhattan. Special alarm: E320, E285, E96, E66, E220, TL 164, TL146, TL 114, L19, TL 135. Fire was on 3 floors of a 41 story office building. This fire went to 8 alarms

11/20/06 1959 hours 2-2 5376 Linden Boulevard and Farmers Boulevard in the Saint Albans section of Queens. Special Call TL 164

10/29/08 0403 hours 2-2-4475 Roosevelt Avenue and Union Street in the Flushing area of Queens. Special Call E325, E286, TL117, TL 164

7/2/12 1127 hours 5-5 4613 60th Avenue and Woodhaven Boulevard, in the Woodhaven section of Queens. TL 164 acting TL138, responded on the fifth alarm

7/26/12 5th alarm fire at box 1015 New York Avenue and Hawthorne Street, in the Flatbush section of Brooklyn. Special Call: TL164 acting L135.

Several Years ago TL 164 was relocated to the north Bronx and was dispatched to the fire as the FAST truck

Following Hurricane Sandy which hit New York on October 29th 2012, Engine 313 and TL 164 were relocated periodically to the Rockaway section of Queens

In January 2014, Engine 313 acting as Bronx Engine 45 responded second due to an all hands fire in the Bronx

These are just a few of the long distance fires, but there have been many more

The guys from E313 & L164 in the old days would never believe it.

FDNY LINGO

I have always found the early FDNY lingo interesting. Some are outdated, others are still in use. Here are some examples that are unique to the FDNY:

A "Job" A working fire

Take a feed: An old expression for breathing in too much smoke

Chauffeur: An apparatus driver

The big house: A double house in the Rockaway section of Queens housing Engine 328, Engine 264 and Ladder 134. In the 1950s the original big house was located in Jamaica and housed Engine 275, Engine 298, Engine 299, Hook and Ladder 127 and Battalion 50

Banjo: A big scoop shovel used to shovel debris or snow

On the job: An insider term for a member of the FDNY

A Bug: This was a very small gold pin that was worn on the sleeve of the dress uniform. It indicated that the wearer had earned a medal for valor. It was a dumb system since no one but another fireman would know what they represented. They have long since been replaced by ribbons similar to the military

The Irons: The axe & halligan bar paired together

"K" Used to indicate the end of the message as in "Notify the police to respond - K"

Rig: Firefighters describing their apparatus

Committee work: A term used for doing routine housework around the station. (I don't know where the term came from, it sounds like something from the old Soviet Union, not the FDNY)

A Bus; A term used for an ambulance, don't ask me why

Proby: New members in their probationary year

1 & 1 or 2 & 2, etc: Short hand for the companies being used for example 1 & 2 means one engine and two trucks are operating at an incident

Still button: Rings the internal bells in the firehouse to turn out the company for telephoned or verbal alarms. There is really nothing silent about it, it seems that the turnout button would be a better name.

Bank down: When smoke fills a room or hallway and banks down to the floor

Can Man: The firefighter assigned to carry a water fire extinguisher

Across the floor: A firefighter transfer within the same firehouse, for example moving from the engine to the truck

Evolution: A uniform sequence of practiced steps used in carrying out common tasks such putting hoses and tools into service

All Hands: A serious fire or emergency when all of the first alarm companies are operating

MD: A radio shortcut for a multiple dwelling

Transmit: As in transmit a transmit a second alarm. This dates back to the days when these signals were actually transmitted over the bell telegraph circuits

Forthwith: Meaning at once, immediately. (This always impressed me as more of an English Lord's word than a firemen's)

AFID: Apparatus field inspection duty

Get Out: An old expression shouted by the house watch to turn out the company

Stand Fast: Companies standing by waiting for assignment

Ripe: A term used to describe a very smoky condition

Engine Three One Three: This would be said as engine three thirteen in any other department

Didn't turn a wheel: No runs on the shift (Don't hear that much anymore)

A hook: Having a friend in high places that looks out for you

Knocked: If during an inspection a uniform or running gear is rejected it is has been "knocked"

Taxpayer: Cheap strip malls built to pay the taxes on the land until the property becomes more valuable

An onion skin: Something temporary or tentative, like a trial period

Mixer off: A radio term used to prevent anyone other than the dispatcher from listening to sensitive information

A verbal alarm: The notification of an emergency received verbally from a civilian

Turn out: A term to describe a company preparing to respond, for example when an alarm is received a fire company will quickly turn out

The members: A term used by firemen to describe the personnel of their company

3 Bagger: An old expression for a third alarm

Doubtful will hold: A radio term used to describe a fire that is not under control

A Grab: An FDNY description of a fireground rescue

Take a blow: Break time on the fireground

Colliers Mansion: A hoarders residence filled with trash and refuse, making firefighting operations and overhaul more difficult. The phrase was coined in 1947 after two wealthy brothers, Homer and Langley Collyer, were discovered dead following a fire in their Harlem home among mounds of newspapers, books, tin cans and rotting trash

Coalition: A gathering of firemen enjoying food and drink following the annual Fireman's Memorial Day or similar event

Roll both companies: An early term used by dispatchers turning out companies by phone

Volly: A volunteer firefighter

Relocation: Used to describe the process of one company occupying the quarters another company to fill a hole in fire protection. Other departments use different terms such as "fill in," "transfer" and "covering"

PD: A radio shortcut for a private dwelling

Jonny: A new fireman with little experience

Take a mark: Take credit for a response

Give it a dash: A burst of water from the nozzle

Da Bronx: Shorthand for the borough of the Bronx

F.A.S.T. Truck: An Acronym for the Firefighter Assist Search Team

Tap us in: Using the firehouse telegraph key to signal that the company was back in quarters from an alarm

The Mainland: The borough of the Bronx

MPO: The motor pump operator firefighter responsible for driving the pumper to the scene of the alarm and operating the pumps

R and R the box: Rewind and reset an alarm box after it has been pulled

The Bag: A term used for carrying correspondence and mail to and from the firehouse

Take up: Pick up your gear and go home

Flash the tin: Showing the badge

Timothy J. Sullivan #3: The FDNY is large enough that more than one member can have the exact same name. The numbers are used to identify a specific Tim Sullivan

The best job in the world: Self explanatory

Through the years some of this lingo has spread to other departments for example the term "taxpayer" is often used by other departments to identify strip mall fires. The holding of 1 & 2 type shortcut is coming into common usage.

EPILOGUE

I moved away from Douglaston and Engine 313 & Ladder 164 in 1960 and it took 20 years before there was a complete turnover in personnel. In the years since I have been in contact with a few of the men from the old days at the firehouse. I called Marty Fetzer Ladder 164 a while back. He was one of the younger men in the station and he was a role model for me. When I was a teenager I bought a shirt like the one he wore around the firehouse. He was promoted to Lieutenant and worked in Brooklyn for a long time where he earned a medal for bravery in rescuing some firemen in trouble. When I called him for old times sake, I told him that I was a voice from the past at Engine 313 and he immediately guessed who I was, I was amazed. I hadn't seen or talked to him in over 40 years!

When I was first promoted to Battalion Chief I visited retired Deputy Chief Mario Cherchi, who lived in Bayside. He was formally a lieutenant at Engine 313 and he was the officer who got me into the FDNY auxiliary. I talked to him about the old days at E313 and asked him about his experiences as a chief officer. Deputy Chief Cherchi recently passed away in January 2013. He was appointed in 1939. At the time of his death he was the fire departments oldest living fireman. He was 98 years old.

There was a Lieutenant Lanahan who was at E313 on a long term detail. I remembered him well as he was much younger than the other officers and he studied all the time. I was aware that he eventually had been promoted to deputy. Years later I was teaching part time at the National Fire Academy and I saw his name on the faculty list and I looked him up. The last time I had seen him he was a young lieutenant and I was a wannabe fireman. The next time I saw him we were both retired Deputy Chiefs. We had a fine time talking about the old days at Engine 313.

About fifteen years ago I was in New York for a family function and I stopped by E313 and met Firefighter Kevin Dempsey. He was very interested in the old days and we had a great conversation and have become friends. I have been corresponding with him through the years and he gave me a great photo from the 1950s of the Engine 313 & Ladder 164 crews lined up in front of quarters that is shown previously in this book. I did not know the picture existed. I was able to identify most of the firemen in the picture as none of them were named. Kevin has since transferred to become a Battalion Aide in the 51st battalion.

My first ride on a fire truck was with Engine 313 when I was about twelve years old, with my bike in the hose bed. Interestingly, my last ride on a fire truck after making 15,000 runs with the D.C. Fire Department was with Engine 313 following the plaque dedication.

I don't get back to Douglaston much anymore. When I am in my old neighborhood I don't know anyone on my block, so naturally I don't expect to see my old neighbors. When I have gone back to my old school, I don't expect to see my old classmates. But, when I stop by Engine 313 I almost expect to see the guys from years ago. I guess that doesn't make sense but thats they way it is. They will always be an important part of my life.

ACKNOWLEDGMENTS

Special thanks to Firefighter Kevin Dempsey, FDNY Battalion 51 (formerly of Engine 313), who provided historical information.

Janet Kimmerly, Editor, WNYF, for providing WNYF copying permission.

Mike Gannon of the Douglaston Historical Society who provided a great deal of information about the Douglaston and Little Neck volunteer fire departments. His grandfather was a member of the Douglaston Hose Company No. 1

Jimmy Raftery FDNY Dispatcher for providing photos including the cover photo.

Lieutenant John Downey, Engine 313, for providing background information.

Ignatius Kapalcznsk who created some of the maps.

Tom Eve, (G man) who provided period assignment cards.

My son Danny, a captain in the Arlington County Virginia Fire Department for his assistance.

My wife Joann for her good advice and support.

APPENDIX

The following FDNY "Walker" firehouses are all identical and were placed in service between 1927 and 1932.

Ladder 3
Engine 205 Ladder 118
Engine 250
Engine 309 Ladder 159
Engine 310 Ladder 174
Engine 321
Engine 38   Ladder 51
Engine 61
Engine 89   Ladder 50
Engine 265 Ladder 121
Engine 302 Ladder 155
Engine 303 Ladder 126
Engine 304 Ladder 162
Engine 311 Ladder 158
Engine 312
Engine 313 Ladder 164
Engine 314
Engine 315 Ladder 125
Engine 316
Engine 317 Ladder 165
Engine 151 Ladder 76
Engine 152
Engine 157 Ladder 80
Engine 159
Engine 162 Ladder 82

The following "Walker" firehouses all similar to the identical firehouses were also placed in service between 1924 and 1931.

Engine 221 Ladder 104
Engine 254 Ladder 153
Engine 318 Ladder 166
Engine 323
Engine 97
Engine 273 Ladder 129
Engine 274
Engine 306
Engine 308
Engine 319
Engine 320 Ladder 167
Engine 155 Ladder 78
Engine 158
Engine 161 Ladder 81
Engine 163 Ladder 83

This information contains copies of original historical documents and period newspaper articles pertaining to the Douglaston and Little Neck Volunteer Fire Departments, all courtesy of the Douglaston Historical Society.

Flushing Daily Times, July 2, 1905

The Douglaston Hose Company No. 1 certificate of incorporation was filed in the office of the Secretary of State on September 13, 1903 and in the office of the clerk of Queens County on September 25, 1903. The land for the Douglaston firehouse was purchased in 1905 from D. L. Van Nostrand and the building was erected by the late William E. Hamilton.

Flushing Daily Times, September 5, 1905

The Douglaston and Little Neck fire companies held a combined parade and games yesterday. A baseball game was played and there was a parade to Little Neck and then back to Douglaston. Games such as dry hose coupling, wet hose contest, tug-of-war, ladder climbing, women's nail driving race, won my Mrs. Raymond Hyde, 100 yard dash relay race, and a potato race. Prizes included desks, watches and cash.

Flushing Daily Times, March 3, 1904

The Little Neck and Douglaston fire companies are considering a proposition to combine the companies. The Douglaston committee considering the proposal includes Denis O'Leary, Walter Faddis, Walter Nelson and Howard Sperry.

Two large rapid firing Gatling guns from the USS Baltimore were unloaded last evening from the L. Boyer Company for delivery to the Douglaston fire company. The guns, probably condemned, were the Hotchkiss patent manufactured by Pratt & Whitney of Hartford, Conn. They were accompanied by eighteen large shells. A member of the Hose Company said that they were to be used for decorative purposes.

Flushing Journal, July 16, 1904

Douglaston Hose Company No. 1 Foreman Adolphus Helmus ordered members out for practice Thursday evening. He intends to have weekly practice as long as weather permits.

Flushing Daily Times, July 2, 1909

The Douglaston Hose Company

Elections:

President Denis O'Leary
Vice-President William Maginnis
Treasurer F.W. Buhrman
Recording Secretary Roby Scott
Financial Secretary Adrlan Van Velson
Chaplain Rev. Albert Bentley
Surgeon Dr. C. Doubleday
Board of Directors:
Dr. J. L. Hawes
William Smith
John Reid
Adolph Helmus
William Harper

Foreman George Graham

1st Ass't Foreman John Hughes
2nd Ass't Foreman William Oberer
3rd Ass't Foreman Lewis Stuart
Steward - Rlchard Baker

Denis O'Leary, President of the Douglaston Hose Company
Member of the U.S. House of Representatives
from New York's 2nd Congressional District

170

DOUGLASTON HOSE COMPANY NO. 1
Douglaston Hose Company mustering out committee
1929

Isaac F. Robinson, Chairman, A.J. McNamara, Chas. Brown Jr., A. Hutton Jr., James Cummings, Gilbert Leek, H. Kaiser, Hon. Denis O'Leary, T. L. Mortimer, William Kershaw, F. D. Hutton, and Chas. F. Mangin

The menu of the last meal of the volunteer fire departments the evening of November 30th, 1929, Little Neck N.Y.

Polly D'Or Inn

NORTHERN BOULEVARD
and ZION STREET

LITTLE NECK, N. Y.

Menu

Celery   Olives

Fruit Cocktail

Vegetable Soup

Filet of Sole   Sliced Tomatoes

Half Broiled Spring Chicken

Fresh String Beans

French Fried Potatoes

Hearts of Lettuce

Ice Cream

Coffee

Douglaston Hose Company No. 1.

List of Members. - all residents of Douglaston.

Name.	Date of Entrance.
Russell L. Boyer.	August 1914
William C. Bilz.	February 1925.
Charles M. Burtis.	October 1922.
George W. Clement, Jr.	December 1920.
James E. Connaughton.	December 1921.
John D. Champlin.	October 1926.
Fred. W. Dane.	December 1922.
Kenneth C. Demlin.	August 1920.
Warren H. Demlin.	August 1920.
Thomas W. Fowler, Jr.	November 1911.
Michael J. Flynn.	March 1923.
Joseph Flynn.	March 1926.
George W. Graham.	August 1904.
A. Edward Graham.	May 1927.
John C. Gabler.	August 1907.
John C. Gabler, Jr.	April 1927.
George H. Gulden.	May 1920.
Andrew E. Gangloff.	August 1915.
Andrew E. Gangloff, Jr.	February 1925.
Frank Gangloff.	March 1926.
Adolph C. Helmus.	June 1917.
Adolph W. Helmus.	June 1921.
Weldon G. Helmus.	March 1925.
John V. Hughes.	September 1906.
Walter Holman.	April 1925.
Albert Humble.	June 1918.
Frank D. Hutton.	May 1915.
George Hamer.	April 1920.
Albert H. Holtzem.	June 1926.
John C. Holtzem.	April 1926.
John Jagnow.	April 1926.
Reuben Kaiser.	March 1925.
William Kershaw.	February 1917.
Patrick J. Knickerbocker.	March 1920.
Harry Levy.	January 1918.
William B. McCurdy.	November 1922.
Fred. Miller.	December 1919.
Frank A. Mortimer.	April 1911.
John W. Mortimer.	April 1911
Joseph J. Mortimer.	April 1920.
Thomas L. Mortimer, Jr.	April 1910.
Edwin J. Mortimer.	February 1920.
Charles Mangan.	December 1919.
John J. McQuade.	May 1920.
S. Oswald Mott.	February 1915.
Joseph J. Nunan, Jr.	October 1926.
William F. Oberer.	May 1918.
Richard T. O'Toole.	May 1920.
Denis O'Leary.	Charter.
Frank J. Page.	August 1910.
C. Kenneth Page.	March 1927.
Dwight Rockwell.	September 1913.
Walter J. Smith.	December 1903.
Henry Sampson, Jr.	September 1911.
Bernhard P. Scheiner.	September 1922.

Douglaston Hose Company No. 1.

List of Members. - all residents of Douglaston.

<u>Sheet No. 2</u>

Name.	Date of Entrance.
Bernhard P. Scheiner, Jr.	April 1925.
Edward C. Seymour.	April 1912.
Peter Szap.	June 1922.
Stephen Szap.	May 1922.
Joseph Spiro.	April 1928.
Frank J. Teague.	June 1917.
Joseph J. Wesley.	June 1911.
Dr. Natheniel P. Breed.	Jul 1915.
James Anderson.	June 1919.

MINSTREL SHOW
and DANCE

by the

DOUGLASTON HOSE COMPANY

Thursday and Friday Evenings
April 18 and 19, 1929

PARISH HALL
DOUGLASTON, L. I.

Douglaston Hose Co., No. 1

Officers

DENIS O'LEARY .... President
FRANK J. PAGE .... Vice President
WILLIAM KERSHAW .... Treasurer
KENNETH PAGE .... Recording Secretary
WILLIAM OBERER .... Financial Secretary

Board of Directors

FRANK J. PAGE, Chairman

RICHARD SMITH   HENRY SAMPSON, JR.

CHARLES MANGAN   ANDREW E. GANGLOFF, SR.

THOMAS L. MORTIMER

Foreman .... FRANK D. HUTTON
First Assistant .... JAMES E. CONNAUGHTON
Second Assistant .... REUBEN KAISER
Third Assistant .... ANDREW E. GANGLOFF, JR.
Surgeon .... DR. N. P. BREED
Color Bearer .... RICHARD O'TOOLE
Chaplain .... REV. R. M. W. BLACK
Quartermaster Sergeant .... HARRY LEVEY
Steward .... FRANK GANGLOFF

PRICE TWO CENTS

Fire Partially Destroys House At Douglaston

Furniture Is Damaged to Extent of About $1000

Crossed Wires Are Blamed For Blaze in L. McGregor Demarest's Dwelling in Centre Drive

Fire which started in the basement and is believed to have resulted from short circuited wires, damaged the furniture approximately $1,000, partially destroyed the three story brick and frame dwelling occupied by Mr. and Mrs. L. McGregor Demarest, on Centre Drive, Douglaston, and drove them out in their night clothes for shelter at 1.30 o'clock this Wednesday morning.

Mrs. Demarest awoke choking with smoke and realizing there must be a fire she called her husband who rushed to the phone and called the volunteer firemen from Douglaston.

Escaped in Their Night Clothing.

They notified the Little Neck Fire Company which responded promptly.

Mrs. Demarest called her maid Mrs. Catherine Rockway, who had not awakened and without waiting to dress the two women took refuge in the home of Mr. and Mrs. Lawrence Clark, next door.

The east side of the house was shooting out flames from cellar to the third story.

The hose was pushed through a cellar window and carried up through the first, second and third floor where the firemen tore away lath, plaster and roofing to get at the flames which had eaten their way up through the partitions of the living room on the first floor, and bedrooms on the second floor to a third story bedroom.

The first story of the house is white brick and the two upper stories of wood.

Compliments Work of Volunteer Firemen.

Mr. Demarest assisted by the firemen removed their piano, oriental rugs, furniture, pictures and bric-a-brac to the sun porch and parlor where they were out of danger from fire, water or smoke.

He later said: "I cannot sufficiently express our appreciation of the work of those fire laddies. They put a hose through the windows and looped back the window curtains so they are not even stained nor is anything smashed."

The Demarests rented the house from the owner, E. Murphy, of 100 Broadway, Manhattan, last April, coming from Brooklyn where Mr. Demarest is with the American Machine and Foundry Company. He said:

"The fire undoubtedly resulted from crossed wires in the basement, quite removed from the furnace. We retired at 9:30 o'clock last evening and the last thing I did was to visit the heating plant where I found everything O. K."

Firemen Showed Much Thoughtfulness.

The damage to the house cannot be estimated as yet but it must be several thousand dollars.

A handsome Tiffany glass window was saved by the splendid efficiency of the volunteer firemen. Their thoughtfulness was noticed when one of them picked up Mrs. Demarest's shoes and threw them into the bushes in the lawn where they were found undamaged this morning.

Roster of Active Hook, Ladder and Hose Company, No 1
of Little Neck, N. Y.
The present officers and members of the company are as follows:

President - Isaac P. Robinson
Vice President - Carl Wannagat
Recording Secretary - Arthur I. McNamara
Financial Secretary - William Kirkman
Treasurer - James W. Fowler
First Assistant Foreman - Gilbert Leek
Second Assistant Foreman - Raymond Williamson

Trustees

James Cummings
John O. Brown
Timothy McQuade
Joseph Hogg
William Stuart
William Brown
Charles Brown, Sr.
Bernard Deneley
William Hutton Sr.
J. H. P. Hervlett
John Munda
Charles Stevens
Frank Szynaka
John A. Brown
George Brown
Charles Bennam
William Hutton, Jr
Howard Hutton
Joseph Munda
John Oska

FIRE DEPARTMENT
44-01 244 STREET   DOUGLASTON, NY 11363
TEL. 718 476-6213   FAX 718 229-4778

ENGINE COMPANY 313

TO: D C Robert Bingham
           304 Jean Place N. E.
           Vienna, Va 22180-3546

FROM: Gary E Stanzoni   Captain

DATE: October 27, 2007

SUBJECT: Letter Of Appreciation

Thank you very much for attending our plaque dedication on Memorial Day October 10, 2007. It was an honor and privilege to have you as our guest.

Thank you for agreeing to speak at our ceremony, your words were inspirational and served to give the members a sense of history. Thank you for a copy of your book, I plan to use many of the points in our daily training.

It was a pleasure to meet you; you will always be an honorary member of Engine 313 & Ladder 164 and The New York City Fire Department. If I may be of any assistance please call anytime.

Fraternally, yours

Gary Stanzoni

Gary Stanzoni

ABOUT THE AUTHOR

Robert Bingham

Robert C. Bingham, a 31 year veteran of the fire service, served as Deputy Chief in the District of Columbia Fire Department, where he was a command officer for 15 years. Chief Bingham is the author of "Street Smart Firefighting." He lives in Vienna, Virginia with his wife Joann. They have been blessed with three children and seven grandchildren.

The author can be reached at binghamrj@hotmail.com